Endors

"Dollar for dollar and hour for hour, the harvest coming from the 10/40 Window nations outstrips that from the rest of the world 100 to 1. That is, if the same money and time spent to win one person to the Lord in the West were put to use in the 10/40 Window nations, the effort would yield a harvest of 100 souls added to the kingdom of God. It is 100 times more cost effective, therefore, to reach those in the 10/40 Window. But for a sizable number of specific ethnolinguistic groups, cost-effectiveness reaches 1000 times more than in Western countries."

David Barrett, *World Christian Encyclopedia*

"God's word declares—His people perish because of a lack of knowledge. *The Move of the Holy Spirit in the 10/40 Window* opens a new door of spiritual fresh air that permeates life, hope, vision, and the necessary challenge for every minister—especially pastors, and then believers in the Body of Christ—to rise up and be a part of what may be the last great harvest. My prayer is that every believer will read this book and enter into a new personal experience with the Lord. It is true—unless something unusual happens now, there will be no hope for the world. 'And God wrought special miracles by the hands of Paul' (Acts 19:11)."

Morris Cerullo, Founder/President, Morris Cerullo World Evangelism

"Luis Bush has been raised up by God as a global trumpeter of a call, passion, and command from the heart of our Lord Himself. Luis writes from the strength of godly character, leadership, and visionary ministry that the Lord has used to mobilize millions to prayer and thousands of Christian workers into missions, and that is resulting in millions of new followers of Jesus. Luis' life and ministry, now joined with Beverly Pegues and hers, offer this book to hope, stir faith, and demand action to complete what Jesus told us to do 2000 years ago—'Go to all the world and preach the Gospel to every creature.'"

**Loren Cunningham, Founder, International Chairman,
Youth With A Mission**

"Here's proof positive that strategic, focused prayer is dramatically impacting that dark and desperate region of the world coined a decade ago by Dr. Luis Bush as the 10/40 Window. *The Move of the Holy Spirit in the 10/40 Window* by Luis Bush and Beverly Pegues is certain to convince the reader that fulfillment of the Great Commission is not only possible, but plausible—and just around the corner."

Dick Eastman, International President, Every Home for Christ

"This book is bursting with hope and packed with challenges to complete the task of evangelization in the least reached areas of the world. It is the story of the sovereign work of God throughout the 10/40 Window."

Paul Eshleman, Director of the *JESUS* Film Project

"Can anyone truly stay home after reading this passionate call to action? Believers will not only be compelled to go, but also equipped to go—with their prayers, their wallets, and their feet."

Elisabeth Farrell, Journalist and co-author, *China: The Hidden Miracle*

"'This gospel of the kingdom will be preached in the whole world' ...not the words of an eager missions promoter, but of the King himself, the only one with the power to make his claim come true! I warmly commend this book, which overflows with stories of the King Jesus bringing his kingdom. May all who read be filled with a longing to find their place, under his rule, in seeking his kingdom."

Leighton Ford, President, Leighton Ford Ministries

"I hate this book—it ruined my mundane life. Unfortunately, it is written by two trustworthy people, so we have to believe them. *The Move of the Holy Spirit in the 10/40 Window* is packed full of information, encouragement, enlightenment, and power: my heart was burning, my mind was racing, and my emotions were racked. I went from smiling to weeping as I read. It devastated me. Without a doubt, this is one of the greatest books on missions ever written. Every seminarian, Bible school student, intercessor, pastor, and church leader should read this book. Frankly, it is a must for every Christian who gives to missions, prays for the lost, or participates in any local church that has a missions budget. This is a hole-in-one for those who love the lost. Beware!"

Ted Haggard, Senior Pastor, New Life Church

"This is a life-changing book! I wept as I read about the sufferings and courage of Christians around the world. It will inspire you to pray, love, and support our fellow brothers and sisters in challenged regions. Luis Bush and Beverly Pegues have touched the heart of God through *The Move of the Holy Spirit in the 10/40 Window*. Every believer should read this book."

Cindy Jacobs, Co-Founder, Generals of Intercession

"This book builds faith in the reader as it inspires us to obey and fulfill the Great Commission. The testimonies and practical examples contained herein will build 'prayer leaders' who, as they then inspire others to pray for the lost of the 10/40 Window, will lay the foundation of God's Kingdom to come on the earth. We have been waiting for *The Move of the Holy Spirit in the 10/40 Window*. It is a must-read for every believer."

Michael D. Little, President, Christian Broadcasting Network, Inc.

"Throughout this decade we have sought to inspire women around the world with the vision of reaching the unreached. This fragile vision is so easily pushed aside by personal needs and local problems, and it requires constant reinforcement.

"At last we have a book that has gathered Scripture, stories, and statistics together to bring the 10/40 Window alive to its readers. And when readers' hearts are broken and their passion level has been inflated with the fire of God's heart for the world, they will find practical ways here to get involved. The end of every chapter offers bite-sized ways and challenging ideas to put their gifts to work for those who have never heard. I can't wait to put this into the hands of the women leaders in our network, so they can march into the 21st century with a renewed and stronger vision."

Lorry Lutz, International Coordinator, AD2000 Women's Track

"It is immensely important to see the nations through God's eyes. This book does that for us. It reminds us that we are living in a time in which we are experiencing the greatest revival in 2000 years of church history. It also invites us to be part of that revival, to help prepare The Bride in every place and among every people for the return of the Son of God. Come quickly, Lord Jesus."

Floyd McClung, Director, YWAM All Nations

"Every once in a while there comes along a concept that is so clear and simple that large numbers of people can grasp it with both hands and put it to good and profitable use. The concept of the 10/40 Window was such a concept, and this mental construct has had a profound impact on how missions is done today. Most books on mission strategy heighten the cognitive component at the expense of the experiential real-life encounter of God's initiative to reach human kind. In this book you will read the stories of many encounters that go beyond the cool rational responses of most missionary thinkers and statespersons. You will in these pages encounter a divine creator of the universe intervening in the affairs of his creation. These stories heighten our awareness of the fact that it is a sovereign God who seeks men and women even today. In his supernatural and modern day interventions you will observe the God of the Bible actively at work in our time. This collection of stories is a wonderful modern day addition to the storied mission histories of the past centuries."

Paul McKaughan, President, EFMA

"This book chronicles the astonishing breakthrough of the Gospel in the power of the Spirit among some of the least reached and most resistant peoples in the world. Bush and Pegues weave instances of the sovereign work of the Holy Spirit into accounts of creative strategy, persistent prayer, courageous witness, and bloody persecution. An informative, encouraging, and challenging book."

Ken Mulholland, Dean, Columbia Biblical Seminary and School of Missions; President of the Evangelical Missiological Society

"There is a fresh wind blowing, not only in areas devoid of the gospel, but also in the face of those whose assumptions would discount the validity of the reports contained in this book. If an Enlightenment mind-set maintains one must suspend belief to entertain such thoughts, perhaps it is time for the church in the West to suspend disbelief in a God who acts in mysterious ways while still gathering to 'worship' that same God."

Bill O'Brien, Director of the Global Center, Beeson Divinity School, Samford University

"You are holding in your hand a very important document giving you a challenging insight into modern missions. It will take you on an armchair tour around the world, providing a bird's eye view of what is happening. You will also meet many individuals, our unknown brothers and sisters, sharing their glorious testimonies of their encounter with the Lord, Jesus Christ. It will cause you to rejoice at what the Holy Spirit is doing in the 10/40 Window today, and it will shock you. It will make you cry to the Lord over the atrocities and persecutions of the many martyrs today, those of our brothers and sisters, of whom the world is not worthy. But most importantly, it will challenge you and move you to take your position in what God is doing. Read this book with an open heart and a willingness to give your personal response to its challenge. What a privilege we have been given to live at the grand finale of the Great Commission. Let us together pray to the Lord of the harvest to send workers into the harvest field. 'And this gospel of the kingdom shall be preached in the whole world as a testimony to all nations, and then the end will come' (Matt. 24:14)."

J. Gunnar Olson, Founder/Chairman, International Christian Chamber of Commerce; Chairperson, AD2000 Business Executives Track

"If you want to know what God is doing in the earth today, you must read *The Move of the Holy Spirit of the 10/40 Window*. Luis Bush and Beverly Pegues have done a masterful job of describing God's revelation of the 10/40 Window approach to world evangelism and the phenomenal testimonies of this evangelistic thrust. Our vision of missions and prayer has exploded since we began to focus on the 10/40 Window. As Jesus' return draws near, we have entered the fierce battle for the souls of unreached peoples. This book will challenge you to join in the fight, giving you strategies for tearing down Satan's final strongholds!"

Larry Stockstill, Senior Pastor, Bethany World Prayer Center

"I believe *The Move of the Holy Spirit in the 10/40 Window* will alert many Christians to the need for world evangelization. This book emphasizes that need by informing the reader about the numerous areas of the world that have never heard the name of Jesus and giving inspiring stories of how the Gospel is being shared in creative ways. It also chronicles the enormous persecution that so many Christians—particularly in the 10/40 Window—are experiencing today. I urge all Christians to take to heart the message of this book, which is to do everything at our disposal—from simply praying to engaging in active evangelism—to make the name of Jesus known throughout the world."

Stephen Strang, President, Strang Communication; Founder, *Charisma* magazine

"Reading *The Move of the Holy Spirit in the 10/40 Window* provides a telescopic view of planet earth from far in space—full of the cosmic wonder of God's special creation, the pain and the glory of the human race, as the marvelous, ultimate triumph of the transforming story of the Lamb. To be reminded again that 'history belongs to the intercessors' is invaluable. The triad of miracles was powerful-conversion, holistic redemption, and signs and wonders. This is a hope-filled book!"

Bill Taylor, Executive Director, Missions Commission, World Evangelical Fellowship

"Luis Bush, my dear colleague, with Beverly Pegues has done it again! Ten years ago, flying 30,000 feet above the earth on our way to Singapore, we talked excitedly about the concentrated area of unreached peoples of the world. Soon after, the term 10/40 Window was coined. Now at the concluding hours of the current century, he and Beverly have given us another shot in the arm: *The Move of the Holy Spirit in the 10/40 Window.* It is a bombshell to our imagination, a boost to our morale, and a testimony of God's mighty hand at work! After reading this account, what we are waiting for? The one word in front of us is *GO!* A must-read document by all Christians. It should be translated and published in every major language in the world."

Thomas Wang, President, Great Commission Center International

"As Daniel prayed through his window toward Jerusalem and God answered, so this book encourages us to pray through the 10/40 Window that God might answer. Through that window we are shown not only the physical and spiritual need but how prayer is opening the window to the breath of God's Spirit, which is bringing new life."

J. Dudley Woodberry, Dean, School of World Mission, Fuller Theological Seminary

The Move
of the
Holy Spirit
in the
10/40 Window

Luis Bush and Beverly Pegues

PUBLISHING
A Ministry Of Youth With A Mission
P.O. Box 55787, Seattle, WA 98155

YWAM Publishing is the publishing ministry of Youth With A Mission. Youth With A Mission (YWAM) is an international missionary organization of Christians from many denominations dedicated to presenting Jesus Christ to this generation. To this end, YWAM has focused its efforts in three main areas: 1) Training and equipping believers for their part in fulfilling the Great Commission (Matthew 28:19). 2) Personal evangelism. 3) Mercy ministry (medical and relief work).

For a free catalog of books and materials write or call:
YWAM Publishing
P.O. Box 55787, Seattle, WA 98155
(425) 771-1153 or (800) 922-2143

The Move of the Holy Spirit in the 10/40 Window
Copyright © 1999 by Luis Bush and Beverly Pegues

Edited by Jane Rumph

Published by Youth With A Mission Publishing
P.O. Box 55787
Seattle, WA 98155

Unless otherwise noted, Scripture quotations in this book are taken from the Holy Bible, New International Version®, Copyright© 1973, 1978, 1984 by the International Bible Society. Used by permission of Zondervan Publishing House.

Verses marked KJV are taken from the King James Version of the Bible.

Verses marked NKJV are taken from the New King James Version, Copyright © 1979, 1980, 1982 by Thomas Nelson, Inc., Publishers. Used by permission.

Verses marked NAS are taken from the New American Standard Bible, © 1960, 1962, 1963, 1968, 1971, 1972, 1973, 1975, 1977 by The Lockman Foundation. Used by permission.

ISBN 1-57658-151-9

Printed in the United States of America.

To the silent heroes who faithfully serve Jesus Christ throughout the 10/40 Window in the face of immeasurable pressure. May His glory be upon you.

Acknowledgments

This book has been birthed out of a realization that the Body of Christ needs to be informed of the wondrous events orchestrated by the Holy Spirit in the 10/40 Window. The compilation of stories, testimonies, and extraordinary occurrences depicted in these pages has been a joint effort by men and women dedicated to reaching the lost with the glorious Gospel of our Lord Jesus Christ.

Many organizations, churches, parachurch ministries, and individuals have submitted information that is in this book. Some of it is from first-hand experience gathered by people actively working on the mission fields in the 10/40 Window. Some information Luis and I have gathered from being in the 10/40 Window or from being in personal contact with workers on the field. Prayer journeyers from around the world saw with their own eyes the marvels God is working in the countries they have visited and told us of their observations.

I (Beverly) would like to thank my good friend, Gabriela (Araya) Spicer, who was with me in Galveston, Texas, where my husband, Leonard, and I went so we could devote time to working on this book. While we were in Galveston, my husband unexpectedly had major surgery. Gabriela's friendship and presence was an encouragement to me to continue on in this most important assignment. She prayed for us and was a faithful companion during one of the most difficult times I can remember.

Chris Moore, part of the "Dream Team" at Christian Information Network, is a dedicated servant of the Most High God. He tirelessly gave of his time coordinating this project and researching the facts you will read in this book. Without his efforts and the efforts of others working at CIN, the task would have been incomplete. I would also like to mention Larry Langley, Barbara Sabol, Bruce Teichroew, and Andrew Mondy who added their labor to see that this formidable assignment was a quality volume.

Jane Rumph, our editor, a professional writer and author, had the enormous task of making final selections from reams of eyewitness accounts, e-mails, faxes, publications, and other documents we sent her and arranging them in a coherent, readable format.

Elisabeth Farrell, also a published author and 10/40 Window prayer journeyer, brought her expertise as a writer and journeyer to this project as well.

Eleanor Taggert was helpful in reading and editing the final manuscript, as was Milan Tellian, whom God has given great wisdom.

I would like to offer a special thanks to my dear friend Tricia Langley. I can still recall her encouraging words throughout the writing process: "Just get it done."

Prayer played a vital part in getting this volume into your hands. My intercessory prayer partners Wanda Elliot, David Russett, Barry Daniel, and Steve Fisher undergirded every aspect of this work in prayer from beginning to end. The New Life Church Tuesday and Saturday Morning Prayer groups who interceded for this project, along with CIN prayer partners, family, and friends, were also essential to the process of producing this book.

Dr. C. Peter Wagner and his wife, Doris, have always been there for me (Beverly) for advice and encouragement. They have played an important part in my life to press toward the mark of the high calling in Christ Jesus.

Ted Haggard, senior pastor of New Life Church in Colorado Springs, Colorado, who is also my boss, has exhibited a love for the lost and missions for many years. He too has been an integral part in getting this gift to the Church finished and into circulation.

Luis Bush, co-author and International Director of AD2000, has spent many years in missions work in the 10/40 Window and elsewhere. His vast knowledge and keen insight into trends in missions helped immensely in the completion of this book. Thanks must also be extended to his wonderful wife, Doris, and his children, Jeannine, Stephanie, Naomi, and Daniel, along with his sons-in-law and grandchildren. Their prayers and support for the important work of reaching the unreached for the Lord has allowed him to concentrate on this important task.

Finally, I would like to thank my precious husband, Leonard, our daughter LaTonya and my mom Norma Tarrant for their love, editorial support, prayers, and encouragement. Even though Leonard had major surgery during the early stages of the writing of this book, he still assisted me throughout the process. It is challenging enough being a wife and mother under normal circumstances. However, when I had to work long hours to complete this labor of love, they were understanding and helpful in so many ways. I couldn't have done this without them.

We acknowledge foremost our Lord Jesus Christ, who shed His blood that we might have eternal life, and the Holy Spirit for the work He is doing in the 10/40 Window today.

It is our prayer that everyone who reads these pages would become actively involved in some way to spread the Gospel to the ends of the earth.

Contents

Foreword

"Goodness, you should put that in writing!"

It is impossible to know exactly how many times I, along with scores of other platform speakers who are reporting what God is currently doing on the mission fields of the world, have heard this statement. The average Christian has never heard anything about the power that God is releasing in the world—especially in the 10/40 Window. It makes the Book of Acts appear to be a mere pilot project. Never before in the history of Christianity has there been a worldwide prayer movement, an evangelistic harvest of souls, and an outward manifestation of supernatural power of the magnitude we have been seeing in the past few years.

No one is more aware of this than Beverly Pegues and Luis Bush. The AD2000 and Beyond Movement, which Luis leads, is the most massive catalytic agency for world evangelism known. The Christian Information Network, which Beverly leads, coordinates the international prayer efforts of the AD2000 United Prayer Track, keeps track of the thousands of prayer journeyers and the millions of home-based intercessors, and tabulates the results. Their data bases have more data and more anecdotes and more testimonies of God's power than anyone else in the world.

They have now done what we have been clamoring for: They have put these marvelous works of God in writing. Now that this book has been published, no Christian leader will lack authentically documented stories to encourage the Body of Christ as to the amazing advance of the kingdom of God in this season. There is enough here to bring life to a year's worth of sermons. No book that I know of could bring praise and joy to the lips of believers like this one can. God is on the throne, and He is exalted on virtually every page of this book!

As you read, you will believe that Habakkuk 1:5 has come to life: "Look among the nations and watch—be utterly astounded! For I will work a work in your days which you would not believe, though it were told you."

Why have such amazing things been happening in the decade of the 1990s that were unknown to previous generations? Beverly and Luis attribute it to the unprecedented amount and quality of prayer that have been ignited on every continent. As you read about the biannual *Praying Through The Window* initiatives; the massive invasion of every part of the 10/40 Window by committed prayer journey teams; aggressive spiritual warfare; powerful prayer for healing the sick, casting out demons, and raising the dead; anointed repentance and reconciliation; the World Prayer Center; and many other spectacular moves of God, you will agree that prayer does truly work.

You and I belong to the first generation since the time of Jesus that can realistically say that it is possible to complete the Great Commission in our lifetimes. By this I do not mean that every human being alive will be saved, but I do mean that "this gospel of the kingdom will be preached in all the world as a witness to all nations" (Matt. 24:14). When (not if!) this happens, it is entirely possible that you and I will be among those privileged to be on station here on earth when the Lord returns!

I can already hear multitudes joyfully saying, "Goodness, I'm glad that Beverly and Luis *did* put it in writing!"

C. PETER WAGNER
World Prayer Center
Colorado Springs, CO

Introduction

The Spirit of the Sovereign Lord is on me,
because the Lord has anointed me
to preach good news to the poor.
He has sent me to bind up the brokenhearted,
to proclaim freedom for the captives
and release from darkness for the prisoners (Isa. 61:1).

Writing a book is a strange process. Although you are reading this Introduction before you begin Chapter One, we are actually writing the Introduction after completing the rest of the book.

Perhaps significantly, during the days we have been writing this book, physical clashes have been raging in the Middle East, North Africa, India, Indonesia, and elsewhere—clashes symbolic of the spiritual warfare raging throughout the 10/40 Window.

No one can predict the outcome of these local skirmishes, but we can predict the outcome of the spiritual war going on in the 10/40 Window. Our mighty sovereign Lord will win—and in fact already has the victory!

They will rebuild the ancient ruins
and restore the places long devastated;

> *they will renew the ruined cities*
> *that have been devastated for generations* (Isa. 61:4).

This book is a report of the glorious work God has accomplished in the 1990s to "rebuild the ancient ruins" in the 10/40 Window. As praise-inspiring as these reports are, if this book ended with them, it would be simply a chronicle of history—and that's not our purpose in reporting them. We want to encourage you—inspire you, motivate you, compel you—to be part of this wonderful move of the Holy Spirit in these last days so that together we can complete the task of preaching the Gospel to every nation, tongue, and tribe.

> *And you will be called priests of the Lord;*
> *You will be named ministers of our God* (Isa. 61:6).

Yes, the Holy Spirit has anointed you to be a priest and minister of our God—to take His name to every corner of the earth. The Book of Acts is the exciting account of how the Holy Spirit empowered a group of fearful, doubt-filled men and women to witness to the ends of the earth. The Book of Acts does not end with chapter 28, however. "Acts chapter 29" continues to this day, and you are part of it!

In his recent book *The Church Is Bigger Than You Think, Operation World* author Patrick Johnstone shows the "remarkable pattern," as he calls it, of the momentum of the past 200 years. In the 1700s, the Gospel traveled across the North Atlantic; in the 1800s, the Pacific; during the 1960s, Africa; the 1970s, Latin America; the 1980s, East Asia; and the 1990s, Eurasia. "The one- and-a-half times encirclement of the globe," Johnstone says, "now leaves us with the challenge of the 10/40 Window area. Central and South Asia and the Middle East are the remaining major areas of challenge" (p. 115).

The 10/40 Window is obviously strategic to the purposes of God and must be to our purposes as well. That's why we encourage you to allow the Holy Spirit to direct you as you read this book. Ask Him to use the reports of exciting victories and heart-wrenching needs to reveal what your part is in proclaiming freedom for the captives in the 10/40 Window.

One major way you can affect the 10/40 Window is through prayer. In recent years, there have been many global prayer efforts, including *Praying Through The Window*, Concerts of Prayer, and prayers focusing on Ramadan and the Hindu world. Prayer is is the foundation of anything we do to reach the 10/40 Window.

Earlier, I (Luis) mentioned that as we are writing this Introduction, many physical battles are raging throughout the 10/40 Window. As we go to press, the Islamic "holy month" Ramadan is underway. Hundreds of millions of Muslims all over the world will pray and fast for thirty days straight.

Brothers and sisters, do we have such dedication to prayer? If 50 million Christians would pray for the 10/40 Window just five minutes a day for thirty days, it would equal more than 14,000 years of prayer! That is fourteen millennia of intercession packed into a single month! Imagine how heaven's golden prayer bowls would overflow with that kind of prayer power. Proactive, powerful, spiritually perceptive, and strategically targeted prayer will exponentially increase the spread of the Gospel in the 10/40 Window. To date, we believe that God has called and blessed the *Praying Through The Window* initiatives to assist the body of Christ in accomplishing this.

God may direct you to become involved with the 10/40 Window in other ways as well. At the end of each chapter in this book, you'll find a section titled "You Can Help Meet the Challenge." Prayerfully and slowly read through each list, allowing the Holy Spirit to speak to you. Obviously everyone can't do everything on every list, but you can do something on some of the lists.

May the Holy Spirit lead you to become increasingly involved in the 10/40 Window—via prayer, advocacy, financial support, prayer journeys, short-term missions, even bi-vocational work or long-term missions. As you become involved, the move of the Holy Spirit in the 10/40 Window will increase beyond anything yet seen.

> *Instead of their shame*
> *my people will receive a double portion,*

and instead of disgrace
they will rejoice in their inheritance...
and everlasting joy will be theirs (Isa. 61:7).

As our dedication shows, we acknowledge the tremendous work that has been done through pioneering missionaries and prayer warriors long before recent prayer movements, partnerships, or alliances were formed. The harvest we reap today is a result of the seed they sowed—many times with their blood. Please remember them as you rejoice in the thrilling reports that follow.

We also ask that you join us in giving all the glory and honor for these victories to the Holy Spirit. We are boasting on the work that He is doing in the 10/40 Window. It's miraculous. It's powerful. It's mind-boggling. It's a sovereign move of God. He chooses to use His children to do these miraculous things, but no church, ministry, or movement can take credit for the wondrous things that are happening in the Window. The credit goes to our wonderful Lord and our precious Holy Spirit. No one else is responsible for perhaps the greatest spiritual harvest of all time.

For as the soil makes the sprout come up
and a garden causes seeds to grow,
so the Sovereign Lord will make righteousness and praise
spring up before all nations (Isa. 61:11).

LUIS BUSH
International Director,
AD2000 and Beyond Movement
Colorado Springs, Colorado

A Word about Verification of Praise Reports

We have sought integrity in reporting the praise reports listed in these pages. Every report and statistic in this book has been verified from primary sources.

1

Commissioned to the Ends of the Earth

*J*esus said in Matthew 28:18–20, "All authority in heaven and on earth has been given to me. Therefore go and make disciples of all nations, baptizing them in the name of the Father and of the Son and of the Holy Spirit, and teaching them to obey everything I have commanded you. And surely I am with you always, to the very end of the age."

Stop and think about this Scripture.

For nearly 2,000 years, the fulfillment of this Great Commission has been a centuries-distant dream for some, a seemingly impossible daydream for others.

Yet consider this. The Lord commanded us to "go and make disciples of all nations." The word *nations* does not refer to countries, which are geographic and political entities, but rather to "people groups" that have their own separate languages and cultures—such as the Kurds, Tung, and Pathan. The Word of God explicitly states that around the throne of God in heaven there will be representatives "from every tribe and language and people and nation" (Rev. 5:9). Dare we believe it possible?

Humankind has seen more change in the past 50 years than in all of recorded history. We have witnessed extraordinary advances in transportation, mind-boggling leaps in information systems, and a virtual revolution in communications technology. Along with these advances, we have skilled armies of missionaries, not only from the West—a vast number of missionaries now come from the Two-thirds World countries!

We have tools that are culturally sensitive to unreached people groups and in many of the known languages. According to May 1998 figures from the International Bible Society, at least a portion of the Bible has been translated into 2,197 languages, with the full Bible in 363 of these. The *JESUS* film, based entirely on the Gospel of Luke, is now available in more than 500 languages, enabling it to be understood by 88 percent of the world's population. More than 1.6 billion (thousand million) people in 223 countries have seen the *JESUS* film, and it is estimated that 83 million people have received Christ as a result of watching it. Moreover, the Lord has blessed the Church with the wealth needed to accomplish the task of reaching the lost worldwide.

The once incomprehensibly vast expanses of planet earth have now been reduced to a "global village." What formerly would have been an isolated and insignificant event in a distant part of the world can now be flashed almost instantly across the television screens of our living rooms through the use of satellite technology.

A single evangelistic campaign can be broadcast around the world and reach hundreds of millions of people from nearly every nation on earth. An important announcement can be made in Israel and watched simultaneously on a television screen deep in the jungles of the Amazon.

Even in highly controlled countries like China, where the government can shut down media channels at a moment's notice, photographs of events like the 1989 massacre in Tienanmen Square can be e-mailed and faxed to every major broadcast company in the world.

What does this mean for believers? God has brought the spiritual needs of unreached people groups to the forefront of His people's awareness and to the top of the Great Commission agenda. He is bringing unity in the Body of Christ as people from different denominations around the globe join to pray and to take prayer journeys among the unreached. More than ever before, churches and parachurch ministries are developing strategic alliances and are networking in unprecedented ways. Today, more believers than at any time in the history of the Church have the expertise and/or field experience to train disciples to become disciplers. In India alone, unprecedented thousands of nationals were graduated from Bible schools in 1998.

In the most technologically modern era of human history, it is inconceivable that the Church has yet to fulfill our Lord's mandate to make disciples of all nations. We still have not reached all of the representatives from each people group who will worship around the throne of God. The declaration of Revelation 15:4 should motivate us: "For you alone are holy. All nations will come and worship before you, for your righteous acts have been revealed."

The Battle for the Window

An estimated 95 percent of the world's unreached people live in an area that is referred to as the 10/40 Window. This spiritually dark region of the world is located 10 degrees to 40 degrees north of the equator, spanning the globe from West Africa through the Middle East and Central Asia to East Asia. The 10/40 Window includes approximately 60 countries. Every major non-Christian religion—Islam, Buddhism, Hinduism, animism, and indigenous religions, as well as atheism—has its headquarters in the 10/40 Window. This area is also home to 85 percent of the world's poorest of the poor.

How many people reside in the Window? A staggering 3.6 billion! This represents two-thirds of the earth's population. Of these, as many as 1.4 billion have never had a chance to hear the Gospel. God is concerned about these billions of people. Therefore, it is crucial for the Church to seek God for His strategy to reach this spiritually impoverished region.

Some observers of current trends in the 10/40 Window feel that the task of penetrating and overpowering the demonic strongholds there seems almost impossible. In 1997 alone, according to the World Evangelization Research Center (WERC) database, 160,000 believers worldwide were brutally martyred. This means that, on average, every day 438 Christians died for their faith, most of them in the 10/40 Window.

While people in North America and other parts of the free world have innumerable opportunities to be exposed to the Gospel, the likelihood of hearing the Gospel even one time in some 10/40 Window countries is almost nil. By the year 2000 it is estimated that more than 77,000 people will die each day in the 10/40 Window without ever having had an opportunity to hear the Gospel message in their own language and in a culturally sensitive way. In India alone, over 23,000 people die daily, many never once having heard the Good News.

It is heart-wrenching to know that more than a billion people may live, die, and eternally perish in the 10/40 Window without understanding God's plan of salvation. In this region the demons of hell have launched a major attack to destroy people whom Jesus Christ died to set free. The 10/40 Window represents Satan's last geographic stronghold. And the battle for the souls of these unreached people is fierce.

Yet the power of our God completely eclipses that of the devil. Now is the hour for the army of the Lord to fight an intense spiritual battle and to seek the release of 3.6 billion souls from the ironclad grip of the powers of darkness. The Church of Jesus Christ must respond to God's call to help the 10/40 Window nations escape the devil's deadly deception.

We are the United Nations task force God will use to bring His salvation message to the perishing, persecuted, and impoverished. God has given us the incredible gift of prayer with which to seek His strategies to reach the 10/40 Window nations. And prayer is a mighty weapon of our spiritual warfare (2 Cor. 10:4).

Burden for Breakthrough

On one of my journeys into the 10/40 Window in June 1991, I (Luis) traveled to Japan, Thailand, and Bangladesh. That trip created an enormous burden in my soul.

During my first night in Bangkok, I witnessed the needs of the city personally. Poverty, prostitution, child prostitution, unsanitary conditions, AIDS, and drugs were everywhere. In the face of such depravity, the words of Jesus in the ninth chapter of Mark took on fresh meaning for me. In that passage, Jesus had come down from the mountain following His transfiguration and encountered a boy possessed by an evil spirit that was robbing him of his speech. The disciples asked why they could not drive out the demon. Jesus replied, "This kind can come out only by prayer" (v. 29).

Revelation of the need for massive prayer for the unreached was driven home to me as I stood in the airport in the city of Chittagong, Bangladesh, preparing to return to Dhaka. Many passengers had flight connections in Dhaka to go on to Mecca for the *hajj,* or Islamic pilgrimage. I watched in amazement as a Muslim stepped up onto a table while waiting for his plane and proceeded to go through his prayer ritual. "What would it take for the spiritual eyes of Muslims to be opened to see that Jesus is not only a prophet, but the Son of God?" I asked myself.

On arrival back in Dhaka, I could not sleep. Finally, I arose and wrote a letter to fax to Peter Wagner, coordinator of the AD2000 United Prayer Track. The date was 13 June 1991.

"It's 3:00 a.m. and I cannot sleep," the letter began. "I have a growing burden to see a spiritual breakthrough and an outpouring of God's Spirit that I must share with you. Peter, if we are to see a spiritual breakthrough and an advance of the Gospel so that the Church is established in the 10/40 Window world by AD2000, it is going to take an enormous prayer and fasting initiative. We need a mighty army of strategic-level prayer warriors saying, 'Lord, give me the 10/40 Window or I'll die.' We need at least one million who are prepared to pray until breakthrough occurs."

The same day I faxed the board chairman of the ministry with which I was involved, seeking early release to give priority to the call of the AD2000 and Beyond Movement and to the 10/40 Window.

The Window Comes into View

My (Luis) intellectual journey through the 10/40 Window began a few years earlier. It came on the occasion of a Christian consultation called Lausanne II, held in Manila in May 1989. Representatives from 170 countries attended. We developed a theme, the "Challenge Before Us." In one of the opening sessions, I learned that most of the world's unreached people groups live in this resistant belt from latitude 10 degrees north to 40 degrees north of the equator, although the region had not yet acquired its own name.

One year later, at the first meeting of the International Board of the AD2000 and Beyond Movement, we struggled with questions. "What would it take to see a church for every people and the Gospel for every person by the year 2000?" Then it hit us like a ton of bricks! "If we are serious about providing a valid opportunity for every people and city to experience the love, truth, and saving power of Jesus Christ, we cannot ignore the reality that we must concentrate on this region of the world."

The evening following the meeting, the many reasons for focusing on that part of the globe began to crystallize. The image of a rectangular-shaped box began to formulate. But what should we call this region? At first it was described as the 10/40 Box. But several months later, awakening one morning to the beauty of a new day and majestic redwood trees framed by our window, the first words that came to my wife, Doris, and me captured a new idea: "Rather than a 10/40 box, why not think of it as the 10/40 Window? A window is a picture of hope, light, life, and vision."

Then in June 1992, a group of leaders met at Every Home for Christ in Colorado Springs, Colorado, to discuss ways to organize a global prayer movement to penetrate the powers of darkness in the 10/40 Window. Intercessors prayed fervently in the next room as the leaders were guided by the Holy Spirit in setting up the foundation for this prayer movement. Ted Haggard, senior pastor of New Life Church in Colorado Springs, volunteered to staff an office in his church to coordinate prayer journeyers and home-based intercessors to pray for the 10/40

Window nations. This became the Christian Information Network (CIN). Pastor Haggard also said he knew the person who should coordinate the prayer effort—Beverly Pegues, who happened to be one of the intercessors praying in the next room.

Things took off from there. The AD2000 United Prayer Track would network with other ministries to develop the *Praying Through The Window* endeavor as we know it today. This endeavor placed a significant emphasis on encouraging believers to form prayer teams to intercede on site in the Window nations. We sought believers from across the globe who were willing to take time off from work with or without pay and raise their own funds to go as God's ambassadors to pray in the Window nations. The participation was surprising and encouraging.

Praying Through The Window

The first *Praying Through The Window* effort aimed to mobilize one million believers to pray for the nations of the 10/40 Window during October 1993. Reports flooded in, and after careful calculation we were amazed that the Lord had raised up more than 20 million home-based intercessors from 28,107 churches in different parts of the world. In addition, 188 prayer journey teams took 257 journeys, visiting most of the Window nations to pray on the soil and ask God for spiritual breakthroughs.

In 1995, building on the prayer momentum of the previous two years, the *Praying Through The Window II* initiative focused on the 100 "Gateway Cities" of the 10/40 Window. The commitment from intercessors exceeded expectation, as more than 35 million praying saints of God participated. Moreover, the number of prayer journey teams more than doubled to 407; the teams took 607 prayer journeys, with 3,000 Christians traveling to most of the "Gateway Cities" to intercede for penetration of the Gospel in those key places.

Praying Through The Window III in 1997 focused on the unreached people groups. This time, nearly 27 million intercessors from 121 nations prayed for the lost of the Window. The 27 million actual participants represent 42 percent of those who originally registered for the prayer campaign. Christian Information Network logged 471 prayer teams that took 563 journeys to the Window countries. Many of the reports in this book come from the observations and experiences of the prayer journeyers who have traveled to the 10/40 Window since 1993.

Praying Through The Window IV: Light the Window will be our final prayer initiative of the millennium. It will culminate in October 1999 when millions of believers across the globe come into agreement while praying through the 31-day prayer calendar. *Praying Through The Window IV: Light the Window* returns to its original focal point of praying specifically for the Window countries, while incorporating the strategic prayer information of the other efforts.

Dr. C. Peter Wagner, coordinator of the AD2000 United Prayer Track and a major visionary behind the *Praying Through The Window* initiatives, has said, "I believe that the principalities over the 10/40 Window are weakening daily, and that the 1999 blow against them will knock down the gates of hell so there will be a church for every people and the Gospel for every person by the end of 2000!"

As Compassion Grows, Commitment Deepens

When believers pray to the Lord of the Harvest to send out laborers into the harvest field, He sometimes sends the very ones who pray. In each *Praying Through The Window* initiative, millions of home-based intercessors prayed in their homes, churches, Bible study groups, and cell groups, over the telephone and over the Internet. Then, by the time we organized the next *Praying Through The Window* effort, many of the home-based intercessors began making plans to become prayer journeyers. Once their hearts expanded with compassion for the needs of the lost, these home-based intercessors were no longer content praying from a distance. They wanted to be part of the hands-on action in the midst of the people for whom they had prayed.

Prayer journeyers say they are motivated to travel to these distant lands because they sense God calling them to go and pray to make a difference among the residents of those lands.

Yet many journeyers experience a surprising phenomenon as they look into the faces of people living in darkness who have never heard the Gospel message. God begins to change *them*, breaking their hearts for the people of the 10/40 Window. The sights, sounds, and smells of the places they visit engage their bodies, souls, and spirits. Upon return, prayer journeyers say that their intercession for those people and places will never be the same because they have left behind a piece of their heart.

Those who travel are not the only ones transformed as a result of prayer journeys. Because intercessors come back with exciting stories about ways the Holy Spirit is moving in the Window countries, they bring fresh vision to their churches. Divine hope arises and stirs congregations to get involved in reaching the 10/40 Window.

One local Presbyterian church in the United States is a good example of the transformation that takes place when a prayer journey team returns. When this church's prayer journey team came back from Turkmenistan in 1997, they shared their experiences during a Sunday evening service. As the congregation listened to the team's stories, they marveled at the conviction they received about the power of prayer and God's mighty hand in reaching the unreached. They soon realized their worldview was expanding to take in more of God's perspective about the lost. Their prayer journey team helped the congregation make the transition from sponsoring a prayer project to engaging in a life of prayer. One church member concluded, "Thanks to the *Praying Through The Window* effort, the missions program of the church has gone from one that was largely confined to less than a dozen members of the congregation to one involving many more."

Through the experiences of the prayer journey teams and their fresh passion after witnessing firsthand the hopelessness in the faces of lost people, the Holy Spirit has ignited a fire among their families and local churches. The Body of believers now has a growing awareness that, like Jesus, we need to do the will of the Father and finish His work (John 4:34). Our prayers can no longer center on our concerns alone. A world to which

God has commanded us to take His glorious message awaits. Consider what Jesus said to His disciples after His resurrection. After the Lord "opened their minds so they could understand the Scriptures," He told them that "repentance and forgiveness of sins will be preached in his name to all nations" (Luke 24:45-47). Praise God that He has a plan for the Gospel to reach the ends of the earth—through us. As with John the Baptist, there is a call on the Body of Christ to prepare the way for the Lord to establish His will in the Window countries.

The Vision Expands Globally

Once the Church becomes informed and begins to pray for the perishing, it reawakens to its responsibility to fulfill the Great Commission. The *Praying Through The Window* emphasis of focusing intercession on the 10/40 Window and sending prayer journey teams is proving to be an effective means of motivating the Church to preach the Gospel everywhere, until every nation knows the glory of Christ's love.

Home-based intercessors who become prayer journeyers have started down an irreversible course that will change their lives forever. Soon many are convicted by a revelation of the truth from Romans 10:14: "How, then, can they call on the one they have not believed in? And how can they believe in the one of whom they have not heard? And how can they hear without someone preaching to them?" Prayer journeyers then begin to cry out, "Lord, I'm willing to be an answer to my prayers. I'll get the training I need. I'll return as a short-term or long-term missionary to help bring in the harvest."

As the Church awakens to the need of the 10/40 Window, many congregations have found their commitment to prayer and missions expanding as never before. An unprecedented number of believers are going on extended fasts, organizing prayer watches, taking prayer journeys, committing to short-term and long-term mission trips, and calling on the Name of the Lord to set captives free.

As a result, many congregations have moved to a new level of involvement in advancing the kingdom of God. These congregations are planting new churches among the unreached and allocating resources into the Window countries. Some church mission committees now evaluate requests for financial assistance with an eye on whether or not the work targets the unreached in the 10/40 Window.

This growth in commitment comes not only from churches in the United States and the West but also from non-Western countries. Even 10/40 Window nations themselves have dramatically increased their number of short- and long-term outreach teams. For example, believers from the Philippines are consciously focusing on sending missionaries and supporting missions efforts in 10/40 Window countries. Already 1,000 Filipino missionaries minister cross-culturally, many in the 10/40 Window. One Filipino minister now pastors one of the largest churches in the Arabian Peninsula. Filipino believers are also having a major impact in the country of Myanmar, as well as in many other spiritually dark lands.

This is not an isolated example. In 1995, Japan—itself a Window country—sent 26 teams to pray in twelve 10/40 Window countries that it once either occupied or went to war against. During the 1997 *Praying Through The Window III* effort, South Africa mobilized more than one million home-based intercessors and sent 30 teams to pray in the 10/40 Window. Furthermore, David Wang, International Director of Asian Outreach, has rallied as many as 25 million believers to pray during the *Praying Through The Window* initiatives. Many of these believers are from Mainland China!

The spreading wave of global involvement in frontier missions outreach has important implications. Because of visa restrictions, citizens of certain countries cannot travel to some of the Window countries. In such a situation, Christians from "neutral countries" can play a strategic role. For example, Arab believers taking prayer journeys into other Arab countries draw less attention than intercessors from the West. The partnership of intercessors and missionaries from the Two-thirds World greatly accelerates the prospect of completing the Great Commission in our day.

Responding to the Call

As I (Beverly) have watched the *Praying Through The Window* initiatives unfold, the passion in my own heart for the lost has mushroomed. After the first *Praying Through The Window* initiative in 1993, several prayer journey teams reported that when their team members asked people if they knew Jesus, time after time people would reply, "I have never heard of that name." Reading these reports caused my heart to grieve. Chills ran through my body to think they had *never* heard the Name of our Lord and Savior—Jesus Christ, the Son of the living God! This seems impossible in our era, when the amount of knowledge available doubles every eight years—and yet millions of people living in our generation still have not been reached with the Gospel message.

Would it be presumptuous to think that God has reserved this era of history to write "Acts Chapter 29"? If there is any time when we need the supernatural power of God working strongly with His Church, it is now. We have God's mandate, the technology, the wealth, and the heart to assure that billions in the 10/40 Window hear a clear presentation of the Gospel in a culturally sensitive manner and in their own language.

A growing number of national and international Christians believe that, if we join forces, the 10/40 Window will be reached in our generation. To do this, we cannot carry on business as usual, especially when it comes to allocation of our financial resources. According to GEM/World Evangelization Research Center, Christian church and parachurch income worldwide totals an estimated US $207 billion, with only US $11.2 billion of that going towards missions. Of the missions dollars, an estimated 87 percent targets those who are already Christians, while another 12 percent goes towards evangelized non-Christians. In other words, only one percent of annual missions resources—roughly one-twentieth of one percent of total church and parachurch income—targets the unevangelized (people who have never heard the Gospel), the vast majority of whom live in the 10/40 Window!

Did God increase the prosperity of the Church so that we would spend the wealth on ourselves and our own desires? Are we in a state of lethargy as we succumb to the craving for our own comfort? The whole Body of Christ must awake to the vast need of the 10/40 Window and remember our responsibility to take the Gospel to the ends of the earth. It is time to unify and bring together kingdom funding and resources to reach this region. The resources are available. The challenge to the Body of Christ worldwide is to invest appropriate finances in the world's area of deepest spiritual need.

The unreached in the 10/40 Window are calling to the Church of Jesus Christ, crying out, "Come over to the 10/40 Window and help us." Let us respond with a reverberating, "Yes, we are coming at once to preach the Gospel" (Acts 16:9-10).

Why Is the 10/40 Window Under Such Strong Influence of the Devil?

One of the most devastating personal and corporate sins is idol worship. The inhabitants of the 10/40 Window live in misery from centuries of bowing down to hundreds of millions of false gods. For generations, they have suffered the consequences of past and present idolatry. The Window countries have been haunted by civil unrest and countless wars, sickness and diseases, extreme poverty, famine, drought, and natural disasters.

Idol worship and entering into demonic pacts have put these countries under the control of Satan. Four of the Ten Commandments deal with God and our relationship to Him. Clearly, our worship is reserved for Him alone, and He will not tolerate idolatry. The Lord instructed the people of Israel in Exodus 20:1-6, "You shall have no other gods before me." He also warned them not to make for themselves any idols or bow down to them. The Lord declares that He is a jealous God and that He will punish us as well as our children for the sins of idolatry that we commit against Him. Herein lies the major problem of the 10/40 Window nations.

The Bible gives clear instruction about the outcome of nations who worship other gods. The consequences are seen throughout the Old Testament, especially in such passages as Deuteronomy 28 and Judges 10:6-16: poverty, disease, drought, famine, plagues, pestilence, disaster, military defeat, foreign invasion, slavery, oppression, confusion. In our day we have witnessed the impact of the curses that fall on nations that fail to worship the one true God.

The Famine in North Korea

The following story from the Spring 1998 issue of *The 10/40 Window Reporter,* written by Drs. Mark and Betsy Neuenschwander, powerfully illustrates this point. The Neuenschwanders are full-time missionary surgeons and founders of International Health Services. They coordinate the AD2000 Crisis Relief Task Force and have established a noodle factory in North Korea that feeds 5,000 daily. They write:

"Where have all the children gone?

"Only three months ago, the children were playing in the streets of Pyongyang, North Korea's capital. Now the streets are almost deserted. Someone said, 'They must be either dead or dying.'

"It was August 1997, and North Korea was in the grip of a devastating famine. To help the starving people, we brought from China 60 tons of flour for making noodles.

"What we saw in Pyongyang made us weep. No children. Factory smokestacks lying idle. By the roadside, gaunt soldiers too weak to move were lying on the ground or shuffling slowly. Obviously the average North Korean was eating starvation rations of 400 calories a day. The maternity hospital in the city had only a two-week supply of oral antibiotics. Another, outside the city, had no medications of any kind!

"Behind the physical signs of famine, we saw spiritual starvation. Everywhere we went, statues and billboards glorified Communist leader Kim Il Sung. At the mausoleum where his body lay in state, we were amazed to see soldiers wiping away tears from their eyes. Although Kim Il Sung has been dead since 1994, they still worship him. At the Children's Palace, dozens of well-fed children jubilantly sang, 'Our great leader has now become our sun.' North Korea's number one problem is that God's provision has been stripped from them due to idolatrous worship of their leaders."

The descent into spiritual darkness

The Neuenschwanders continue: "Sadly, Pyongyang is far from what it was at the turn of the century. In 1910, a great revival took place there. In fact, people called the capital city the 'Second Jerusalem.' After Japan annexed Korea in 1910, the persecution of Christians began. As the Japanese watched the Korean Christians rapidly grow in number to 96,000 by 1914, they considered them a threat.

"Japan began to impose its religious beliefs, a mixture of Shintoism (ancestor worship and belief that spirits and gods dwell in nature) and Buddhism. The most powerful deity was the sun goddess. In fact, the Japanese believe their emperor became a god himself when he made a covenant with the sun goddess. For them, patriotism and emperor worship became one and the same. This they imposed on the Koreans.

"By 1937 or 1938, Shinto shrines, each containing a picture of the Japanese emperor as god, blanketed the entire Japanese empire, including Korea. The Japanese ordered all Christian school students to worship at Shinto shrines. Rather than submitting, the Presbyterians closed all their schools while the other denominations chose to conform. They rationalized that such worship was an insignificant 'cultural rite.'

"Then in 1938, the ultimate horror occurred! The Japanese not only demanded that all Christians appear at a Shinto shrine before attending their own church services, but they also ordered Shinto shrines to be built on all church property!

"Finally, the Body of Christ fractured. On 11 September 1938, the Presbyterians, the last to succumb to political pressure, advised their members to bow at Shinto shrines as their 'civic duty.' A few years later, after the end of World War II, the Communists took over North Korea, and it sank into the pit of atheism."

The spiritual roots of a physical problem

The Neuenschwanders conclude: "Paul writes that 'The god of this age has blinded the minds of unbelievers...' (2 Cor. 4:4). Christians of South Korea, Japan, and America hold the keys for bringing God's deliverance and blessing to the North Koreans. God says, 'I take no pleasure in the death of the wicked...' (Ezek. 33:11).

"We must remember, as Ephesians 6:12 says, that 'our struggle is not against flesh and blood, but against the rulers, against the authorities, against the powers of this dark world and against the spiritual forces of evil in the heavenly realms.' We can use our delegated authority in Jesus' Name, apply the Blood of Jesus, persevere in prayer, and render ineffective the evil one's grip on North Korea. As we pray, God will raise up the leaders and policies of His choice, as he did in Daniel's time.

"This is a crucial time for Christians to respond with acts of love and kindness. It is our Lord's command to us to restore lands and redeem nations (Isa. 58:10–12). 'This is how we know what love is: Jesus Christ laid down his life for us. And we ought to lay down our lives for our brothers' (1 John 3:16)."

Satan the Destroyer

Because of the curses and consequences of idolatry, the devil has free reign to steal, kill, and destroy wherever worship of false gods prevails. John Robb, director of the Unreached Peoples Program for MARC (Missions Advanced Research and Communication Center), a division of World Vision International, writes on this theme: "Satan... [is] dedicated to destroying human beings made in the image of God. Satan is the master deceiver and the author of idolatry, seeking to dominate the world by undermining faith in God, twisting values, and promoting false ideologies. He does this by infiltrating institutions, governments, communications media, educational systems, and religious bodies, and uses these to seduce humankind to worship money, fame, success, power, pleasure, science, art, politics, and religious idols."[1]

No inhabited region on earth is immune to the destructive schemes of the devil. But the areas most ravaged by Satan's evil forces correspond to sectors of entrenched worship of false gods. Demonic forces often turn their human captives against one another in unrestrained violence.

We see examples in our news media regularly. In the Himalayan state Jammu and Kashmir, Muslims and Hindus have been battling for years to control the area. More than 15,000 deaths have been attributed to the fighting since 1989. An Associated Press report from September 1997 was headlined, "Muslims Rampage to Avenge Mosque Burning." After a battle between Indian troops and separatist insurgents destroyed a 15th-century Muslim shrine in Srinagar, India, riots broke out among those bent on revenge. The angry crowds burned schools, government buildings, and Hindu temples; fires then spread to the town and destroyed 1,500 homes and businesses. Two months later an attack instigated by radical Islamists killed 66 people, mainly tourists, at Hatshepsut temple in the Egyptian Valley of the Kings near Luxor. Reuters news service reported that since 1992 more than 1,100 people have died in Egypt during efforts by militants to topple the secular government and install a pure Islamic state.

This kind of demonically inspired strife occurs not only between religious factions, but also within the same faith. In India, violence between Hindu castes has raged over issues of justice and traditional subservience. While the nation's constitution outlaws caste discrimination, the system of social hierarchy remains common in rural areas. A 2 December 1997 report from the Associated Press describes how 61 low-caste Hindus, including 19 teenagers and four preschool children, were massacred during the night in Lakshmanpur, 580 miles southeast of New Delhi in Bihar state. Local police blamed "an illegal militia of mostly upper-caste landowners who terrorize villagers who dare question their supremacy."

Only the Gospel of Jesus Christ can free people from the devastation caused by worship of and enslavement to the forces of darkness (Jer. 10:11-16). No other region is under greater bondage to these forces than the 10/40 Window.

We Are Called and Commissioned

Now is the time for the Body of Christ to come to grips with these questions: Is our God worthy of worship, adoration, and praise? Do we sincerely believe that the Lord is more powerful than Satan and his army? Is God really concerned about the lost and their plight? If we answer "yes," we have a mandate from God to combat the forces of idolatry holding the 10/40 Window in bondage. We must take the Gospel message, with the Holy Spirit's power, to the Window nations as the Apostle Paul did—"not with wise and persuasive words, but with a demonstration of the Spirit's power, so that [the] faith [of the Window nations] might not rest on men's wisdom, but on God's power" (1 Cor. 2:4-5).

The Church of Jesus Christ has been commanded by God to go and take back the defiled land and to carry the Good News to the ends of the earth. We see this powerfully illustrated throughout the Book of Acts. The apostle Paul, called and commissioned by God, took three missionary journeys throughout 19 provinces of the ancient world. Interestingly, many of these areas lie within the 10/40 Window.

The ancient Church had its roots in this now spiritually dark area of the world. But the Church lost its authority in this region where Christianity once thrived. How did this happen? The Church grew weak, complacent, and self-absorbed. While the Church focused on itself and failed to reach out to those who did not know Jesus Christ, the enemy infiltrated the region. Now the challenge has been passed to a new generation. We must rise up and take the Gospel to these desolate lands. It is our responsibility to lead the captives out of captivity. We must exercise our God-given authority over the powers of darkness.

The Lord said in John 14:15, "If you love me, you will obey what I command." As we draw close to the Lord, we will sense

His broken heart for the people of the 10/40 Window. As mentioned earlier, by the turn of the millennium it is estimated that more than 77,000 people in the Window nations will die daily. Unless we reach them with the Gospel, they will plunge into a Christless eternity in hell.

The Challenge to the Church

The Church has numerous obstacles to overcome in order to fulfill the Great Commission. As Christians we must be willing to give generously, not only of our finances and material resources, but also of ourselves, our time, and our expertise. The Great Commission demands proper stewardship of all these resources. Prayer and prayer journeys, as well as short- and long-term missions trips, require time. Moreover, commitment to the cause may prove dangerous. We must be willing to lay down our lives, and even the lives of our children, to accomplish the evangelization of the 10/40 Window people.

Radical obedience by the Church will overcome these obstacles. Our generation must arise and take the initiative to reach the 10/40 Window, a burgeoning harvest field in desperate need of laborers. The Window nations need our help. Jesus Himself, before He can return in triumph, awaits our full obedience to His mandate (Matt. 24:14).

The Bible gives us models in which believers overthrew the powers of darkness and took back defiled land. God promised Moses and Joshua, "Every place where you set your foot will be yours" (Deut. 11:24; Josh. 1:3). The Old Testament tells of foreigners who learned to worship and believe in the God of Abraham, the God of Isaac, and the God of Jacob. In the New Testament era, the kingdom of God advanced even further. Jesus gave the gift of eternal life to the Samaritan woman, and Paul preached to the Gentiles. Empowered by the Holy Spirit, Jesus went into foreign territories, and the people flocked to Him. As the apostles preached the Gospel near and far, the Lord added believers to their number daily.

According to Acts 14:16, God at one time let all nations go their own way, but now He is drawing them to Himself. This is true in the 10/40 Window today. The Father is concerned about the people in the Window who do not yet have a personal relationship with His Son. It is their turn to hear this Good News, and our responsibility, according to Jesus' commission in Matthew 28:18-20, to bring it to them!

Will we go? Will we take up the challenge? Are we willing to minister to the needs of some of the world's neediest people? Consider the words of author Mike Mason: "If man really is fashioned, more than anything else, in the image of God, then clearly it follows that there is nothing on earth so near to God as a human being. The conclusion is inescapable, that to be in the presence of even the meanest, lowest, most repulsive specimen of humanity in the world is still to be closer to God than when looking up into a starry sky or at a beautiful sunset.

"Other people, let us face it, confront us directly with the reality of love or hate that is in our hearts in a way that all the beautiful sunsets in the world cannot do."[2]

May God place in each of our hearts His passionate love for the lost and perishing in the 10/40 Window!

You Can Help Meet the Challenge

- Ask the Lord if His purpose for your life has to do with reaching the 10/40 Window nations.
- Pray daily for the 10/40 Window nations.
- Find out names of missionaries and servant ministries working in the 10/40 Window. Support them financially and with prayer.
- Support church-planting efforts by providing Bibles and discipleship training materials.
- Ask the Holy Spirit to give you and your church creative ways to serve the 10/40 Window nations.
- Pray that God will send more harvesters into the harvest field.
- See "Organization and Ministry listing" at the end of this book for a list of ministries to network with.

- Contact Christian Information Network about taking a prayer journey into the 10/40 Window:

>   Christian Information Network
>   11005 State Highway 83 North, Suite 159
>   Colorado Springs, CO 80921-3623 USA
>   Telephone: (719) 522-1040
>   Fax: (719) 277-7148
>   E-mail: cin@cin1040.net
>   Web Site: www.Christian-info.com

Endnotes

1. John Robb with Larry Wilson, "In God's Kingdom...Prayer Is Social Action," *World Vision* magazine, February–March 1997, p. 4
2. Mike Mason, *The Mystery of Marriage*, Portland, Oregon: Multnomah Press, 1985, p. 38

2

Signs, Wonders, and Miracles Empower the Church

*L*imba screamed in agony as the demons swarmed at him, taking over his body. His family came running and watched helplessly as, yet again, Limba's tortured frame writhed under the evil spirits' attack. The family members could not see the scene that filled Limba's vision—thousands of demons that seemed to mob him and chop him up. But as the spirits entered Limba's body, his family saw his flesh swell like one grossly obese.

As the son of the village chief in Dhuliagarh, India, a village in the district of Banswara, in southern Rajisthan, Limba grew up tormented by demons because his father was also a prominent witch doctor who practiced demonic rituals. In his father's hut was a seat made of human ashes picked from cremation sites. As the years passed, Limba came under increasing bondage.

Limba's father tried unsuccessfully to deliver his son from his torment. He called his circle of friends, but they could not free Limba either. So they took Limba on a Hindu pilgrimage in the hope of cleansing his soul. That effort failed.

They then took Limba to the temple of the monkey god next to the Mahi River, near the famous Mahi dam of Rajasthan. By this time the young man was bedridden, seriously ill and existing as though half dead. A strange, sickly smell issued from his body. His family was told to walk seven times around the temple and place Limba in the holy bath.

Still nothing happened. The Hindu priests said that Limba's case was hopeless. They advised Limba's father to throw him into the river to get rid of him so that his soul might merge with the big spirit of the river. His father, however, brought him home.

Then two evangelists from Every Home for Christ (EHC), Laugi and Gaugi, came to the village as part of their literature distribution process. They learned that Limba was sick and immediately went to his home. There they found a crowd already gathered, expecting Limba to die soon. When the evangelists saw him, they lost heart. Limba's pathetic body lay convulsing in the throes of death.

Suddenly a ray of hope pierced their hearts. They watched with amazement as Limba came to his senses for a moment. He started shouting, "Doctors, sir, please heal me, because I see many big black giants coming to cut me into pieces." The evangelists understood that, beyond Limba's physical sickness, the powers of darkness were snuffing out his life.

Laugi and Gaugi turned to the crowd that had gathered. With brevity and clarity the evangelists shared with them about Jesus Christ. They asked the people to believe what God could do and to join them in a prayer of faith for Limba.

The moment they prayed with that authority, Limba fainted. Stinking water oozed out of his pores, like juice from a boiled tomato that is squeezed. Within a few hours, Limba's swelling subsided as the demons that had once possessed him fled.

In the wake of this healing and deliverance, Limba lay in bed recovering from general weakness. On the seventh day, without anyone teaching him the word, he shouted, "Hallelujah!" and began praising God. People thought he had gone mad, but in fact he was being filled with the Holy Spirit.

Limba's life was transformed by the Spirit of Christ. Like young Timothy to the apostle Paul, he became a disciple to Gaugi and Laugi. He trained and volunteered with EHC until 1993, when he became a missionary. Limba has been serving the Lord now for twelve years.

I (Luis) met Limba and Gaugi during the Rajasthan Harvest Consultation in Jaipur, 19–21 July 1998, where I heard Limba's astounding testimony personally. Now, if Limba does not see a miracle each day, he questions his life in the Lord. Although he is still basically illiterate, he has 15 disciples as well as spiritual ownership and responsibility over a group of villages in the Dhuliagarh area. His own people call him *maharaj,* or priest.

Limba's story is just one of many reports of miracles and power encounters in Rajasthan, especially among the Bhil tribe. And India has no monopoly on signs and wonders today. Countless contemporary stories from across the 10/40 Window and the rest of the world could come right out of the Book of Acts.

Miracles Are Both Effective and Insufficient

Around the world God is responding to the prayers of His children in supernatural ways. Doors are opening to the Gospel that seemed impossibly closed. God is using healings, miracles, dreams, visions, angelic encounters, and other divinely sent phenomena to bring not only individuals but entire families and even villages to faith in Jesus Christ.

In many lands where a cognitive explanation of the Gospel might hit a wall of resistance, a demonstration of God's love and power through a supernatural sign can break through intellectual barriers to pierce the heart. Scales fall off spiritually blind eyes when people see, perhaps for the first time, that God is real, that He knows and cares personally about them and their urgent needs, and that He is willing to intervene for them.

In the 10/40 Window the forces of darkness have reigned for centuries. Inhabitants of that area know full well the existence of the supernatural realm. For many, religion is not so much an issue of truth as an issue of power. They will worship the deity who demonstrates the greatest power. As believers have come to realize this and pray for God's power to be demonstrated, signs and wonders in the Name of Jesus have multiplied across mission fields all over the world, ripening an unprecedented harvest.

But will miraculous signs be enough? Can we afford to pray for miracles and neglect the groundbreaking work of crossing cultural barriers with the Gospel message? Clearly, supernatural signs were not enough for Old Testament Israel. The God who chose Israel out of all nations parted the Red Sea so that they could flee from Egypt on dry land. He satisfied their hunger by raining manna from heaven for 40 years and quenched their thirst by providing water from a rock. Many of their battle victories depended on divine intervention, including a storm of hailstones on their enemies and a delay of sundown for almost a full day. Yet many Israelites rebelled against God and the truth of His law.

New Testament Pharisees had hearts just as hard. Jesus acknowledged this when He told the parable of the rich man and Lazarus, "If they do not listen to Moses and the Prophets, they will not be convinced even if someone rises from the dead" (Luke 16:31).

God does not perform miracles simply to amaze or astonish us. His ultimate goal is reconciling men and women to a relationship with Himself. He doesn't demonstrate His omnipotence indiscriminately if a sign would go unheeded. When He knows, however, that a supernatural touch of His divine power will enable the Holy Spirit to penetrate the heart of a lost soul and bring that person to faith in Christ, then He in His relentless love will not hesitate to do whatever is needed to accomplish this goal.

The Apostle Paul gives us an effective model as he describes how he combined communication of the Gospel message with signs revealing God's might: "Our gospel came to you not simply with words, but also with power, with the Holy Spirit and with deep conviction" (1 Thess. 1:5).

The stories in this chapter illustrate how the Holy Spirit is demonstrating the saving power of God throughout the 10/40 Window. Let these accounts boost your faith in our Almighty God and spur your prayers for more supernatural break-throughs among those who have yet to hear and respond to the Gospel.

ALBANIA:
Healing Follows Vision of Jesus

Josua Dienst, a German mission agency, reports that many Albanian Christians tell of extraordinary protection during the civil war: "Liri Peqini's 18-year-old son was shot in the chest, and the doctors at the hospital had no hope that he would survive. His mother and many other Christians prayed day and night, and after four days, he was out of bed. He says that Jesus appeared to him in a vision while he was in the hospital. The doctors are amazed."[1]

CHINA:
Deaf and Disabled Woman Healed through Teenager's Prayer

Pastor Dennis Balcombe of Hong Kong recently said that more than 8 million Chinese become Christians and are baptized each year. He says that the motto of the Chinese Christians is "Woe is me, if I do not preach the Gospel."

One example: Fourteen-year-old "Anna" (name changed) was saved in Inner Mongolia. Full of excitement, she wanted to go immediately to preach the Gospel, but because of her age she was put together with another Christian 20 years older. One day, they started talking with a farmer on her field, who told them that she had no time but said, rather emotionally, "Go into the house and speak to the old woman lying in bed."

Anna went in and spoke of the Gospel with this old bedridden woman, who constantly nodded as though she understood what she was hearing. Suddenly, the farmer came into the house and shouted at Anna, "She can't hear you; she is deaf!"

But Anna replied, "No, she hears me. Jesus can heal people, and He healed her!"

The farmer was not satisfied and said, "If Jesus can really heal people, then make Him heal her of her disability. She hasn't been able to get out of bed for years."

Excited, Anna replied, "Yes! Yes! Of course He can heal her!" She ran to the old woman, took her hand, and slowly pulled her to stand up. When she was upright, the old woman started slowly to walk around. Because of the miracle, the entire family decided to become Christians, and now they have a house church in their home.[2]

ETHIOPIA:
God Raised Her from the Dead in Welega

"My name is Haptamu, and I live in southern Ethiopia Ledant and run Rhema church some 600 kilometers from Addis Ababa. We had heard that one of our Christian brothers' sisters was sick. When we reached the village she had died. We asked to be shown the body. We went to where she lay and began to pray for her. All the people around, upon seeing us praying, loudly began to scream and fell down manifesting demons, for there is much witchcraft practiced in these parts. We had to stop praying and deliver the people from these demons. When they were all cast out, we returned to the business of praying for this woman. After praying we laid hands on her and her life returned, and she sat up. We fed her some food, for she was hungry. She was healed and delivered—praise God!"[3]

Assayehegn Berhe, General Secretary of Evangelical Church Fellowships of Ethiopia reports, "Such a happening as a miracle of raising from the dead is normal in Ethiopia...We have seen God in action like [in] the early church of the New Testament."

GAMBIA:
Vision of Jesus Brings Turnaround in Muslim Man

A prayer journeyer writes: "One team member witnessed to an ardent Muslim who was adamant about his religion. Two days later the Muslim ran up to the same person and excitedly told him he'd had a vision of Jesus. Jesus showed him the nail prints in His hands, pointed to him, and told him to follow Him. The Muslim gave his life to the Lord."[4]

INDIA:
"Jesus Is the Only True God; He Healed My Son."

Little Manjunath, Lakshmi's only son, was suffering with jaundice (from hepatitis) and not responding to any treatment. Lakshmi, dejected, lost all hope that he would live.

Lakshmi did not know what to do. As she wondered how her son's life could be saved, some of her friends urged her to go to Chitra Kalai. They had confidence that the God whom Chitra Kalai worshiped was powerful. Chitra's neighbor told Lakshmi that if she would go to Chitra's house, they would pray to the Lord Jesus Christ who would heal her son.

Lakshmi was prepared to do anything, if only her son's life would be spared. Lakshmi carried the little boy and walked a couple of kilometers from Hormavu to Kalkeri, hoping that this effort would bring healing to her boy.

Chitra was greatly shocked to see the desperate condition of the mother and explained to her clearly the way of salvation. She also explained that she herself had no power, but that the Lord Jesus Christ alone could hear her earnest prayer and heal her little Manjunath.

Lakshmi listened intently and said that she would certainly place her faith in the Lord Jesus Christ if her son were healed. Chitra prayed that the Lord would be merciful to Manjunath and heal him.

Jesus heard the earnest prayer and touched the lad. Manjunath was healed, and Lakshmi placed her faith completely in Jesus. With joy beaming over her face, she returned to Chitra's house to thank her for praying. "Yes, Jesus Christ is the only true God. He healed my son," said Lakshmi, who confessed that she had given her heart to the Lord and would follow Him only.

Lakshmi has openly shared her faith in Jesus with her husband, and she regularly attends the Sunday worship services and the women's meetings on Fridays.[5]

Blood of Jesus Inspires Life-Changing Dream

Rajeer was born into the revered Pujari caste of Hindu priests who offer prayers and sacrifices to the gods on behalf of the people. He was proud of his heritage. When a team of Every Home for Christ (EHC) workers knocked on his door in Secunderabad, Rajeer listened politely as they shared the Gospel and accepted their invitation to come see a Christian film in the village center that evening.

While Rajeer was unconvinced by the testimony of the EHC workers or by the Christian film, when he went to sleep that night his dreams told a different story.

"That night I dreamed a strange dream," Rajeer recalled. "I saw the water vat in our house filled with blood. Then somebody took me by the hand and dipped it in the vat. I felt great joy and found that I was cleansed."

Rajeer went on, "Immediately I got up from my bed and ran to the missionaries in the early hours of morning and shared my joy. They confirmed that Christ Jesus wanted to cleanse me and save me. So I asked the missionaries to baptize me because I accepted Jesus as my personal Savior and Lord. On that day my daughter, Bhagyamma, and I took baptism. Today, all my village wonders how a Pujari like me turned out to be a follower of Jesus Christ."

The seeds of the Gospel being sown by EHC workers in India have resulted in more than 6.77 million responses from people like Rajeer and have led to the formation of 19,963 village Christ Group fellowships. Praise God for the great move of the Holy Spirit in India.[6]

Church Planting with Prayer and a Bucket of Water

A new Christian, an ex-Hindu, was shocked. His rice field was full of weeds. Because his harvest looked so poor, he was in danger of becoming the target of village jokes. In tears, he went to the Indian missionary Ravikumar Kurapati.

"I encouraged him with the Word of God," says Kurapati. "The next day, I went with him to his field, watched by almost the entire village. I took a bucket of fresh water, and prayed. I then asked him to take the water and throw it over his crop. When the harvest time came, he was amazed. He collected an incredible 30 sacks of rice from his narrow strip of land. It also opened the other villagers' eyes to see that Jesus Christ is the true God," says Kurapati, who planted a new church in the village. With a thankful heart, the farmer donated some of his land for the church.[7]

Hindu Baby Healed after Prayer Journeyers Intercede

"Our prayer journey to Varanasi started with an overnight stay at Kachuwa Christian Hospital, 30 minutes from Varanasi. Our team spent most of the day in fellowship and some time in worship with the hospital staff. Two of our team members were nurses. They had a great interest in touring the hospital compound and learning more about the practice of medicine in the Third World.

"At the start of the tour, our two nurses were approached by hospital staff asking them to come and pray for a baby, one or two years old, who had been very sick and who was now having trouble breathing. They agreed to pray for the baby when they arrived on their tour to that part of the hospital. They did not realize that the tour would turn into a teaching seminar and formal introduction to every hospital staff member, with a visit to every closet in the place. They came to the baby and mother four hours later.

"The hospital nurses told them, 'You have waited too long; it is too late.' The baby was gasping for every breath and everyone was certain the child would not live through the night. Doctors and nurses were not able to diagnose the problem. Our nurses prayed with the mother for the baby and assured her that if the baby got better, the reason would certainly be Jesus.

"After the prayer, our nurses left and returned to the team, very upset that they had not responded immediately to the call to prayer. They again prayed with four other prayer journey team members.

"The following morning, before the team departed for Varanasi to pray, they anxiously sought news of the baby. The baby, they learned, was sitting up in bed—crying, laughing, and doing baby stuff with the mother! Totally healed by Jesus, the baby and mother were released from the hospital that evening."[8]

Crippled Man Healed, Church Planted

Dr. Sam Thomas, head doctor at the Herbertpur Christian Hospital in Dehradun at the foot of the Himalayas in the Indian state of Uttar Pradesh, told us of new evangelistic breakthroughs.

The village of Andheri, 140 kilometers away from the hospital, is located in Himachal Pradesh, an almost completely unreached state with 5.5 million inhabitants and fewer than 100 known Christians. The village's head man experienced how his second son was healed through an operation at the hospital and prayer by Christians. He invited the hospital team to visit his village. A doctor's visit is very exciting for such a remote village, so the news of their arrival spread quickly.

Men from another village in that area brought a severely crippled man whose legs were set in a sitting position. To bring him to the doctor, they had to carry him over three mountains in a basket. Dr. Thomas examined the man; his diagnosis filled the man's friends with hopelessness. But when Dr. Thomas prayed for the man in Jesus' Name, the man was healed before their eyes.

Since then, a church of 35 to 40 members has been started in Andheri. Seven churches have been planted in recent years due to the hospital's evangelistic work.[9]

"God, What Should I Do Today?"

Ramesh, an ex-Hindu, became a Christian through the work of Herbertpur Christian Hospital. "I have been persecuted and avoided, simply because I became a Christian," says Ramesh. He now gets up at 3 a.m. daily to pray and ask God what he should do that day.

One day, God told him to go to a particular village. Ramesh thought, "I've already been there. I'll go to another one." On the way, though, he asked himself, "Why should I follow my flesh?" He then went to the village God had shown him.

When he arrived, he spoke to a woman outside her home who was interested in the Gospel, but her husband came and chased him away. He went on to the next house, but the woman followed him secretly because she suffered from very strong headaches. Ramesh gained insight into the woman's condition when he prayed for her in Jesus' Name. He candidly stated that she was being tormented by a demon—which then vanished after prayer, along with the headaches.

As a result, the woman's husband and many other villagers came to hear what Ramesh had to say about Jesus. Ramesh has been able to lead many people to become Christians.[10]

Teenager Returns from Death to Tell of the True God

The Malto tribe live in the north of India, in the state of Bihar. The people are resistant, even hostile, to the Gospel. The area is saturated with the worship of Satan and hundreds of false gods. The people know it is Satan, the great evil god, who oppresses them. On occasion, our Sovereign Lord uses extraordinary means—miracles—to penetrate enemy strongholds and validate His truth.

A *JESUS* film team approached the Malto tribe. But the resistance was so strong that they bypassed the area and went on to more receptive villages. A few days later, a 16-year-old girl died in one of the Malto villages.

It was evening, and the family had finished all the preparations for burial. Many had gathered around to pay their respects and support the family. They were about to bury the body when the girl suddenly, miraculously, awoke.

In stunned disbelief the people told her, "Then you were not dead!"

"Yes, I *was* dead," she told them. "I went to the place of the dead. But God told me I must come back and tell you about the real God, the true God."

Still astonished, the villagers began to ask her, "Then who is the true God?"

She went on to tell them it was the God proclaimed by the film teams they had turned away. "God has given me seven days to tell as many people as I can that He is real," the girl said.

The next day, she sought out and found the *JESUS* film team in another village. She told them her story and said that

God had told her she was to go with them. For the next seven days, they showed the film to the now receptive Malto villages. (Needless to say, word had spread everywhere about her return from death!) Before every crowd, she fearlessly proclaimed, "I was dead, but God has sent me back to tell you that this film is about the true and living God. He has given me seven days to tell you. You need to believe in Him."

Then, after the seventh day, although she appeared fine physically, the girl collapsed and died.

"Now, I can't offer you any proof that she was really dead," says Dr. Thomas of Herbertpur Christian Hospital. "There was no death certificate, as we know it. I cannot explain, theologically, all the circumstances. However, I can tell you that even the most unsophisticated people (by Western standards) do know how to recognize death—especially in someone who has been dead several hours."

The significant fact of the entire situation was the boldness demonstrated by this young girl. She had a powerful sense of mission. She sought out and traveled with the *JESUS* film team, even willing to suffer persecution. Without fear (she knew she would die after the seventh day) and with unrelenting determination, she brought this message to her people. The greatest evidence that something wondrous happened is that during those seven days, hundreds of people who were bound by the chains of Satan turned to the living Christ. As a result, at least six churches were established. Certainly, God was glorified![11]

Christ Saves New Believer from Hot Coals

Eight families in India's Bihar province were ready for baptism, but the village leader—an unbeliever—wanted one believer, a man named Sandhu, put to the test of standing on hot coals. While other believers prayed, Sandhu calmly stepped onto the coals and stood there for ten minutes. Forty-seven villagers accepted Christ that day. Thank God for glorifying His Name by again delivering His people from the fire.[12]

Six-Year-Old Boy—Among Others—Raised from the Dead

Dunger is a village on the border between the northern Indian states of Rajasthan and Gujarat. A six-year-old boy drowned there recently and was to be buried later the same day, as is normal in many countries with warm climates.

However, according to Parthing Matchar, the boy's father, members of the Indian Pentecostal Church (IPC), including Pastor Duad, a Christian named Manu, and a number of others, arrived before the burial. They prayed in Jesus' Name and symbolically placed their Bibles on the child's body. "Then the child opened his eyes, alive. We could find no words to express our feelings as we experienced God's power raising the dead as He did in Acts."

Delhi Pastor K. Y. Geevarghese, president of one section of the Indian Pentecostal Church, confirmed not only that Pastor Duad has recently seen four people raised from the dead, but also that his movement has planted 110 churches in Rajasthan and 123 in Haryana, both North Indian states traditionally almost unreached.

Pastor Geevarghese explains their method of church planting this way: "Jesus' power is again and again demonstrated as our pastors and evangelists travel to the villages, and we regularly experience healings, deliverance from demons, and people being raised from the dead."[13]

Deliverance and Salvation amid Opposition

"At first, Randeep didn't want to pray for the girl. She was lying on the ground, possessed by demons, and the Hindu Pujari (witch doctor) wanted money and goats to drive the spirits out. God spoke to Randeep: 'If you don't pray for her, I will ask someone else.' Randeep obeyed, prayed, and the girl was delivered. The people were greatly shocked.

"The next morning, others came to knock on Randeep's door, asking him to pray for them as well. Thousands heard the Gospel. Many people were freed from demons and repented of their sins, and a church was born.

"Then came the opposition. Randeep was captured and hung head down over a river with his feet tied together. He was told that he would be drowned if he did not promise to leave the district. He quietly replied that they should let the rope down, because he would not leave. His persecutors decided not to drown him. Instead, they stabbed him in the stomach. He didn't have to go to the hospital, however, because Jesus healed him. Randeep's young wife told him, 'If you die for the Lord in Kinnaur District [Himachal Pradesh], I will raise our son and pray that he will take your place.'"[14]

Local Hindu Politician Raised from the Dead

Raju (name changed) was a newly-saved Christian who listened carefully as his pastor spoke of the healing miracles Jesus performed. The stories became reality for him as a tumor from which he suffered vanished before his eyes. His personal experience of how Jesus is healing people today caused his faith to grow dramatically.

A few days later, Raju passed through a village in Rajasthan, where he heard that a local politician belonging to the fanatic Hindu party RSS had just died. Raju offered to pray for the dead man. The dead man's relatives told him to go away, but Raju insisted that Jesus can raise people from the dead. He pushed his way through the people and laid his hands on the dead man's body.

As he prayed, the man's hands started to move, frightening the others present. With that, Raju became even more bold. Turning to the others, he told them that they must declare that Jesus is Lord and Savior of all people before he continued to pray. Everyone present did so, and as Raju continued praying, the dead man rose in front of their eyes. As a result, all of the politician's family members decided to become Christians.[15]

IRAQ:
Miracles Happen Often

Ali (name changed) lives in northern Iraq, in the region he calls Kurdistan. In his own words, this is his report of signs and wonders he has seen: "I come from a Muslim family, but have repented and now believe in Jesus Christ. He is the God of my life. The number of Christians in Kurdistan is growing. Only seven months ago, we met once each month, and now we meet twice a week. We serve the Lord Jesus and lead others to Him. The number of believers is growing every day.

"Since my conversion, two of my sisters and a cousin have also become Christians. Many of us are persecuted by our own families. We often experience miracles. I had a knife wound in my chest that the doctor told me would take three to four years to heal, but it has already healed after only a year, because of prayer.

"Suleyman, a friend of mine and a guerrilla in one of Kurdistan's political parties, once saw my Bible. I gave him a copy and led him to Christ two days later. He was suffering from a stomach ulcer. After a while, I took him to a Christian church where they prayed for him. Within a day his ulcer had disappeared!

"Ibrahim also experienced a miracle. He became ill and lost his memory. He could not remember who anyone was. One Wednesday we prayed for him. Four days later on Sunday, he came to church completely healed. He is now learning about computers, and translated this letter into English for me!"[16]

KUWAIT:
Seven-Year-Old Sees Jesus and Is Healed

Babu Govind, who grew up in a Hindu family, became a Christian in 1993. His seven-year-old son, Ajith Babu, was diagnosed as suffering from retinal pigmentation in December 1995. Ajith had completely lost the use of one eye and could see only 30 percent with the other. Doctors had given up all hope.

"As a family, we started praying intensely," Govind writes. "On the fifth day, during our devotions shortly before mid-night, my son saw Jesus come down to him in a fire, with angels standing on each side. Jesus looked at Ajith and said, 'Son, never sin.' Ajith then saw a dark, skeleton-like figure behind him, who quickly left because of Jesus' presence. Afterwards, my son was completely healed."[17]

MALAYSIA:
Hindu Finds God While Meditating

One day while meditating, Suresh, a strict Hindu, heard the words, "I am the way, the truth, and the life," but he had no idea who spoke to him and why. For three days, he heard the same voice speaking the words. He asked a Christian acquaintance about this, who took him to a Catholic priest. The priest showed him the verse in the Bible (John 14:6) that he had heard. Suresh then knew that it was Jesus who had spoken to him, and he decided to become a Christian. Today, all the members of his family are baptized Christians and members of the Anglican St. Christopher's Church in Ulu Tiram.[18]

MIDDLE EAST/NORTH AFRICA:
Radio Show Helps Muslims Interpret Dreams

One of the top pastors in Egypt and a Christian psychologist got together to tape the first show of a radio program called "The Joseph Hour."

Many in North Africa and the Middle East are having dreams and visions confirming the reality of Christ. After one radio program reported that Jesus had appeared to many Muslims in a dream and said to them, "I am the Way," the radio station received thousands of letters in which the listeners said they had suddenly understood their earlier dreams. They wanted more information about Jesus.

God once before changed an entire country through a young man who could interpret dreams—Joseph. He told Pharaoh's officials that the interpretation of dreams belongs to God (Gen. 40:8). Why should that not happen again? The radio program aims to help Muslims understand correctly their spiritual needs by interpreting their dreams.[19]

MONGOLIA:
Sick Healed amid Great Openness to the Gospel

An eyewitness report states: "There were many healings as we prayed for the sick. As days passed, more and more would show up for our meetings to be prayed for as word spread. This all happened by word of mouth, since Mongolia is still restricted and we could not advertise or speak outdoors without being arrested.

"We prayed that the Mongolians and Tuvans would have open hearts to the Gospel. The Lord truly answered this prayer. Everywhere we went people were open to the Gospel. One older woman who was considered a very strong Buddhist, who had called monks into her house to curse the Christians she knew about, came to one of our house church meetings. She accepted the Lord as her Savior. The problem is not in reaching the lost but in discipling them, because there are so few strong Christians."[20]

SRI LANKA:
Healing Brings Buddhist to Christ

Pastor Jayalath of Waragoda, Kelaniya, reports what God recently did in his church in Sri Lanka. "On the second Sunday in March 1997, the relative of one of the church members, a fiery Buddhist, came to our service. He was a reporter and a religious writer who was active in trying to spread Buddhism. He was very ill. His lungs were heavily congested and he had great difficulty breathing. He received prayer in Jesus' Name and was healed. X-rays taken in Colombo's Nawaloka Hospital show that the healing is complete. The man is now a committed Christian."[21]

THAILAND:
Healed of Epilepsy; Half a Village Saved

In a special ceremony, a Thai couple filled a bottle with rice, hair, and fingernails and then prayed to evil spirits to protect their son as he grew up. The opposite happened. The child became chronically ill, suffering from epilepsy. Raewat, a Thai missionary on a long tour through the jungle and rice paddies with two assistants, arrived in the village. The missionaries knew they were the first Christians ever to visit the village, because the villagers were completely speechless as Raewat preached there. The villagers' lives were full of evil spirits who had to be placated with endless rituals. They had never heard of a God who loved people.

The missionaries also met the epileptic boy's parents. As the missionaries prayed for him, God acted immediately and healed the boy. When the parents saw what had happened, they destroyed the magic bottle and burned its contents. Afterward, other people from the village burned their amulets and other instruments that they had used for Buddhist and animist worship. "Most of the villagers confessed their sins and decided to become Christians," according to the report.[22]

Prayer and Fasting Bring Rain and Salvation

The lack of rain had almost ruined crops in Thailand's Kalasin province when a village leader interrupted a worship service to ask the Thai missionary to pray for rain. The leader pledged that all the village's 134 families would accept Christ if the rains came. The believers prayed and fasted for three days. The fourth day brought an intense cloudburst that flooded the rice fields. Praise God for those who came to Christ—and continue to come—as a result.[23]

You Can Help Meet the Challenge

- Praise the Lord for ways He is showing His mighty power to open the eyes of the lost to Jesus Christ.
- Intercede for more breakthroughs as the kingdom of God advances against the kingdom of darkness.
- Pray that God would answer the prayers of non-believers in the Window countries who want to receive dreams and visions by giving them dreams about Jesus.
- When a non-believer you know experiences a blessing through a sign or wonder or miracle, acknowledge Jesus as the source and share the truth of who He is.
- Be ready to pray boldly when the Lord gives you opportunity to minister to someone who needs a supernatural touch from God.

Endnotes

1. Source: Nick Wakely, Elbasan, Albania, via Josua Ministries, 19 August 1997; reported in DAWN Friday Fax #36.97, 12 September 1997

2. Source: Dennis Balcombe, *China Report,* January 1997; reported in DAWN Friday Fax #8.97, 28 February 1997

3. Source: Russell White, 24 January 1998; reported by Awakening e-mail list

4. Source: Name verified and withheld; YWAM; prayer journey report, 21 November 1997, p. 2

5. Source: India for Christ Ministries Newsletter, Madanapalle Mission Field, Andhra Pradesh

6. Source: Every Home for Christ newsletter, 20 October 1997

7. Source: Gospel for Asia, Thiruvalla, India; reported in DAWN Friday Fax #44.96, 15 November 1996

8. Source: Name verified and withheld; prayer journey report, 21 November 1997

9. Source: Dr. Sam Thomas, Herbertpur Christian Hospital, Uttar Pradesh; reported in DAWN Friday Fax #7.97, 21 February 1997

10. Source: Ramesh, via Dr. Sam Thomas, Herbertpur Christian Hospital, Uttar Pradesh; reported in DAWN Friday Fax #7.97, 21 February 1997

11. Source: Paul Eshleman, November 1997 *JESUS* Film Report

12. Source: *Advance* newsletter, March 1997

13. Source: K. Y. Geevarghese, Indian Pentecostal Church–W.C.R., Delhi; reported in DAWN Friday Fax #43.97, 7 November 1997

14. Source: North India Harvest Network (NIHN)/Concern; reported in *PrayerNet Newsletter* of the U.S. Prayer Track, 17 October 1997

15. Source: Rev. Rajamani, Mission Director of the Assemblies of God Churches in India, Madurai; reported in DAWN Friday Fax #20.97, 23 May 1997

16. Source: Compass Direct; reported in DAWN Friday Fax #27.97, 11 July 1997

17. Source: Mr. Babu Govind, Khaldhuya, Kuwait; reported in DAWN Friday Fax #14.97, 11 April 1997

18. Source: J. S. Thomas, Malaysia; reported in DAWN Friday Fax #12.97, 28 March 1997

19. Source: Wolfgang Simson, e-mail of 15 August 1998

20. Source: Name verified and withheld; Faith Christian Center/Reachout 2000, 28 April 1997

21. Source: Pastor Jayalath, Waragoda, Kelaniya; reported in DAWN Friday Fax #30.97, 1 August 1997

22. Source: Gospel for Asia, India/USA; reported in DAWN Friday Fax #33.97, 22 August 1997

23. Source: *Advance* newsletter, April 1997

3

God Is Greater Than the Powers of Darkness

The powers of darkness run rampant throughout the 10/40 Window. Physical calamities, human conflicts, and spiritual bondages claim lives every day, lives that Jesus died to save. Amid unceasing news of death and despair, it would be easy to give up hope that the kingdom of God will prevail. Is there any hope? Yes, thank God! Our God is greater than the powers of darkness.

In late 1997, a believer we will call Fred, who had been working as an expatriate in an Arabian Peninsula nation, prepared to return to his home country. He had finished his professional commitments and planned to fly out the next day.

Fred went to visit a local believer and friend we will call Omar to say his last good-bye. Not long after Fred arrived, another young man—a committed Muslim—dropped by. The timing seemed a bit premeditated.

It didn't take long to get into a discussion of religion. As the three of them sat together on the floor, Fred and Omar shared the Gospel with the Muslim for about 45 minutes.

Then the Muslim visitor asked Fred, "What do you think of Islam and Mohammed?"

Fred answered carefully that in light of everything he had just discussed—the need for a blood sacrifice and the forgiveness of sin—he did not think that Islam was true or that Mohammed was a true prophet.

Incensed, the Muslim rose to his feet. As he confronted Fred, their conversation took on a high pitch. Omar felt things getting out of hand and slowly stood up.

At this the visitor reached behind his back. He pulled out a pistol and, only four feet away, pointed it at Fred's head.

Omar tried to lunge between Fred and the gun, but he was too late. The Muslim pulled the trigger. *Click!* Nothing happened. He pulled the trigger again. *Click!* Nothing. The gun had misfired twice.

Suddenly the young Muslim's face filled with fear, and he ran out of the house. Fred and Omar sat down to pray, thanking God for His protection and interceding for the young man's salvation.

The next morning, the day of Fred's departure from the country, his telephone rang.

"I must see you!" Omar begged his friend.

Omar arrived a short time later and explained what had happened the night before. The Muslim man had come back to Omar's house during the night and burst into tears. He told Omar that he had gone home very confused.

"I thought I had the protection of Allah," the young man said, "and that I would be doing Allah a favor by removing this man from the earth. I didn't understand. How could this blasphemer have been protected by Allah? I thought maybe something was wrong with my gun. So I went outside and pointed the pistol at the ground. I pulled the trigger again, and it fired perfectly!"

The young man told Omar how he had gone back into his home and thought through everything he had heard about Jesus. He relived what had happened when he tried to kill Fred. Finally, he decided to return to Omar's house.

As Fred listened, Omar continued, "He confessed to me that he was too ashamed to go see you himself, so he wrote you this letter. Over and over he asked for your forgiveness. So he wrote you a letter because he wanted you to know before you left that he now believes all the things we told him. He now believes in Jesus Christ, the Messiah, as his Lord and Savior forever!"

Our source for this remarkable story—kept confidential but personally verified—rejoices at the move of the Holy Spirit in the midst of circumstances that are difficult and life-threatening.

Often, the same circumstances the devil intends for evil God uses for His good purposes. Free-lance writer Elisabeth Farrell, who reports frequently on the church in China, shared with us a wonderful example:

"During the Cultural Revolution 30 years ago, China's Chairman Mao required that every citizen learn Mandarin. Prior to that, Chinese spoke many minority languages that made it difficult for people from one region to communicate with the people from other regions. Mao, of course, was an evil dictator who inflicted years of brutality on China, yet his decree that everyone learn Mandarin has now made it easier to evangelize China. Mao also built roads for the army, which Christians now travel to evangelize the country. Mao kicked out missionaries, shut the country off for ten years, and killed or imprisoned most of the Christians. This persecution, however, strengthened the underground Chinese believers, and they grew in numbers. The Church that flourished was completely Chinese. No one could ever again claim that Christianity is a foreigners' religion."

Satan's Wrath and God's Victory

Demonic activity has a long history in the 10/40 Window. Some believers feel that the Church lost its authority in the 10/40 Window when Christians of the early centuries failed to reach people around them with the Gospel message. Could the disarray experienced by the Church in the past be the main hindrance to a major spiritual awakening among the people in the 10/40 Window today?

This spiritually desolate part of the world has been plagued with significant demonic influence, manifested in tyrannical governments. Numerous wars have brought famine, poverty, sickness, and calamity. The concept of the sacred worth of human life finds little acceptance in the 10/40 Window. Satan continually unleashes his wrath on God's people, with persecution against Christians now increasing rapidly. More oppression and suffering occur among believers in the 10/40 Window than anywhere else in the world.

Satan's deception of Adam and Eve began the vicious cycle of sin and evil. Because of our sin, the devil currently holds sway over the world (1 John 5:19). Humankind experiences wars, hate crimes, persecutions, evil of every sort, and disasters caused by earthquakes, hurricanes, tornadoes, floods, famine, epidemic sickness, and diseases. Can there be any doubt that this physical evidence shows Satan's opposition to the kingdom of God?

Yet the ultimate victory of God in redeeming the world is not in question. The Word of God says that Satan is filled with fury because he knows his time is short (Rev. 12:12). He knows that the Church has been given authority as the Lord's agent to take the Gospel to the ends of the earth. Further, the Church is pressing in to fulfill Jesus' declaration that "this gospel of the kingdom will be preached in the whole world as a testimony to all nations, and then the end will come" (Matt. 24:14).

While Satan fights fervently to oppose the advance of the Gospel in the 10/40 Window, the Church of Jesus Christ can take hope. The Lord Himself has declared that we will prevail against the powers of darkness (Matt. 16:18).

A Vision of God's Vast Power

Intellectually we know that God is greater than the powers of darkness. The One who spoke the universe into existence and made humankind as the crown of His creation on the sixth day rules over everything, including created spiritual beings. Yet amid the evil surrounding us in this world, we sometimes struggle to believe this truth wholeheartedly.

One weekend the Lord gave me (Beverly) insight about this truth. I was having some health problems at the time and was sleeping a lot. Every time I went to sleep, I would have a recurring dream, and each time the Lord would add to the scene. I dreamed that I stood above the earth looking down on the 10/40 Window countries. I saw the limitless vista of stars and planets spread out before me. I had a tremendous bird's-eye view of the universe and remember thinking, "This is only a portion of God's vast creation." The great creative ability and awesomeness of our God touched me deeply.

Then, suddenly, I realized that the Lord was ever so slightly behind me. I could see His majestic robes in my peripheral vision—robes in beautiful shades of purple and gold, made of fabric that shimmered like flowing water.

The Lord said to me, "Beverly, look on the ground and find a grain of sand."

The idea of me being able to do this from such a great distance seemed impossible. Finally I said, "Lord, I won't be able to find a grain of sand from this distance unless You show me."

Instantly the Lord zoomed me to an unknown seashore and showed me an individual grain of sand. I reached down and picked it up. It was amazing.

Then He said to me, "Beverly, this is how much power the devil has compared to My power." As I thought about everything the Lord had shown me above the earth and realized my authority in Christ Jesus, I threw that piece of sand down and started stomping on it.

The Lord, however, cautioned me. "Beverly, a single grain of sand can cause blindness and irritation to the eyes so that you cannot see the things of God clearly."

What a time I had with the Lord that weekend! I learned in a graphic way that, while the devil's power is not to be trifled with, God's power is infinitely greater and able to overcome the blindness, bondage, and misery caused by demonic forces throughout the world.

Repentance As a Spiritual Weapon

Intolerance of religious differences characterizes the 10/40 Window nations. Within this vast region, Hinduism developed some 4,000 years ago and Buddhism originated in the

5th century BC. With the introduction of Islam in the 7th century AD, and finally the savagery of the Christian Crusaders who swept across Europe and the Middle East beginning in the 11th century, the stage was set for generations of religious competition, mistrust, and bloodshed.

The Word of God proclaims, "We are human, but we don't wage war with human plans and methods. We use God's mighty weapons, not mere worldly weapons, to knock down the devil's strongholds. With these weapons we break down every proud argument that keeps people from knowing God. With these weapons we conquer their rebellious ideas, and we teach them to obey Christ" (2 Cor. 10:3-5, NLB). Using these mighty, spiritual weapons, including the power of repentance, Jesus Christ and His Church will obtain final victory over the devil and his dark kingdom.

In 1009, the "Mad Caliph," Al-Hakim, destroyed the Church of the Holy Sepulcher.[1] On 27 November 1095, the Christian Church decided to wage war as humans do. In an inflammatory sermon, Pope Urban II stirred his congregation to recapture the Holy Land from the Muslim Turks, sparking the First Crusade. Thus began one of the darkest events in the annals of history. Religious fervor was not the only motivation for the Crusades. Men were promised riches and lands if they would liberate the birthplace of the Savior and shrines of the saints from the followers of Mohammed.

The First Crusade was unprecedented in the history of religious persecution. Instead of accomplishing the conversion of the "infidels," the Crusades had the opposite effect. Jesus said that His kingdom was not of this world, but by using military means to rid the world of unbelievers, Crusaders negated the message of love that the early Christians preached.

For the past nine hundred years, the land has been invaded countless times, with thousands of people killed and displaced. Jerusalem, the "city of peace," has seen little of the peace it so desperately seeks. Reconciliation leaders in coalition with many others are now dealing with this issue through the Reconciliation Walk. The Reconciliation Walk is an international movement to retrace in humility all known routes of the First Crusade, with walkers bearing to Muslims, Jews, and Orthodox Christians a message of repentance for the atrocities inflicted by Crusaders against their ancestors in the Name of Christ. Since Easter Sunday 1996, teams of Christians have walked through cities and villages in Europe and the Middle East, asking forgiveness for the corporate sins of the Church and seeking reconciliation. A solemn assembly of repentance is planned when the teams enter Jerusalem on 15 July 1999, exactly 900 years after the bloody massacre committed by the Crusaders.

Intercessors on the Walk carry a message written in several languages that reads in part, "We wish to retrace the footsteps of the Crusaders in apology for their deeds and in demonstration of the true meaning of the Cross. We deeply regret the atrocities committed in the name of Christ by our predecessors. We renounce greed, hatred, and fear and condemn all violence done in the name of Jesus Christ."

When the Walk began in 1996 in Cologne, Germany, the team asked permission to visit the local mosque and present the printed message of apology. The Imam (leading teacher) granted consent, but the intercessors still felt apprehensive as they approached the mosque. Lynn Green, International Director for the Reconciliation Walk, later wrote:

"When everyone was settled on the carpeted floor, the Imam officially welcomed us. Then I explained that we had come to apologize for the atrocities committed in the name of Christ during the Crusades. The reading of the message of apology in German, Turkish, and English was greeted with loud, sustained applause.

"Then the Imam, who understood and spoke all three languages, responded: 'When I heard the nature of your message, I was astonished and filled with hope. I thought to myself, "Whoever had this idea must have had an epiphany, a visit from God himself." It is my wish that this project should become a very great success.'

"In further private conversation, he told me that many Muslims were beginning to examine their sins against Christians and Jews. He said that our example would show them how they could do something about the sins of the past. As we parted, he promised to send the message out to their 250 mosques in Europe."[2]

Not only does the Reconciliation Walk seek to make clear to Muslims that deeds done during the Crusades were an abomination against followers of Mohammed, but it also addresses crimes committed against those of the Jewish faith and against other believers who were not in the Crusaders' religious camp. Seyyed Hussein Nasr, a Muslim and professor of Islamic Studies at George Washington University, stated, "Every effort by both sides to bring Christians and Muslims closer together and to unify them before the formidable forces of irreligion and secularism, which yield inordinate power today, must be supported by people of faith in both worlds."[3]

The Price May Be High, but No Nation Is Beyond God's Reach

The clash of spiritual powers is especially evident in the North African nations. While the enemy pushes hard against the Church there, the Holy Spirit is giving strong anointing in the midst of God's people. Despite war, famine, enslavement, and persecution of Christians, a mighty move of God is in progress, much of it empowered by the grace of the believers to endure suffering and forgive others.

Heart-wrenching stories have filtered out of the region about Christian villages being burned and believers being forced into refugee camps. Eyewitness accounts from these camps of the horrors perpetrated on Christians are shocking and inconceivable. The methods used to force captive Christians to convert to Islam include torture, starvation, endless recitation of the Qu'ran, and bribery—with offers of jobs, lands, homes, and marriage to those who convert.

Young Christians have difficulty finding Christian mates in such a culture. These young people stand on the Word in their determination not to be unequally yoked with unbelievers. They know that their strong stand may mean that they will never marry. However, like believers in many 10/40 Window nations, they are willing "rather to suffer affliction with the people of God, than to enjoy the pleasures of sin for a season; esteeming the reproach of Christ greater riches than the treasures" offered to them by their tormentors (Heb. 11:25–26, KJV).

Accounts of horrific persecution are coming out of Sudan. One man reported that when his brother became a believer in Christ, Islamic fundamentalists came to the home of their mother, tied her up, placed her in the middle of the floor, and forced her to watch the fate of her son. They attempted to persuade the new believer to renounce his faith. When he refused, he was stabbed repeatedly until he died.

The brother and sister of the murdered man vowed revenge. But God moved in the mother's heart immediately to forgive her son's brutal murderers. Her family and friends were amazed that she did not want to avenge her son's death.

Later, in a church service the brother attended, the Holy Spirit swept through the room and commanded him to forgive the murderers and to pray for their salvation. He resisted the Lord's voice. Yet the Spirit of peace persisted. Eventually, the Lord enabled him to forgive. Now he is praying for the salvation of the men who killed his brother. Once more we see the overwhelming demonstration of the power of God that enables us to perform feats beyond our human capacity. Forgiveness is a powerful weapon in breaking the stronghold of demonic forces.

Even in the most difficult situations, God is able to intervene and accomplish His purposes. During the second week in January 1998, a week-long biannual event called Christian Family Convention was held in Sudan's capital, Khartoum. On the first night, 12 January, some 7,000 people gathered to hear the message of Jesus' love and salvation. The next night the number grew to more than 11,000. An estimated 15,000 attended on the following night. In total, thousands came forward to receive prayer. Many received Jesus for the first time in their lives. Others were filled with the Holy Spirit, healed of diseases, and freed from demonic spirits. Only the bookkeepers in heaven know how many people were added to the roll of believers that week!

Christian leaders attribute these radical changes in Sudan to prayer. They extend their thanks to those outside their country who are praying for Sudan.

In the North African nation of Algeria, reports from confidential but verified sources tell of God's protection of His people. In one town that has suffered because of armed conflict between the government and radical Islamists, a 30 member underground church has taken root. In the first weeks of April 1998, 21 people were baptized.

The 10/40 Window Reporter gives this report: "Suspected arson by extreme militants destroys Christian bookstore in Amman, Jordan. The fire on 27 January 1998 was the latest in a series of attacks on the bookstore, following an evangelistic outreach last summer. Jordanian officials suspect these attacks to be the work of 'an extremist, highly militant group.' The latest fire destroyed the shop's books, videos, and most of the office equipment and files. The bookstore contained the largest Arabic/English library of Christian videos (about 300) in the Middle East. Estimated damage loss ranged between US $20,000 and $30,000."[4] The owners publicly announced that they forgave the arsonists and were praying for them. They later reopened the bookstore after a major rebuilding project.

Bob Havenor, the former senior pastor of Christ Community Church in Colorado Springs, Colorado, took a prayer journey team to the Bako region of Mali. They learned about a local shaman with occult power to turn himself into an animal or even, some insisted, a whirlwind. During the team's prayers a Fula man lingered nearby, later asking how to repent of his sins. Havenor tells the story: "Baba Kone, a Malian pastor, shared the Gospel with the Fula man. As Baba began to lead the man in the 'sinner's prayer,' a ferocious wind kicked up, blowing dust and debris everywhere, virtually stopping the prayer. Kevin Walzak and I both realized this was the [demonic] whirlwind. In Jesus' Name we commanded it to cease. Immediately all was calm.

The prayer continued, and a concerned Fula inquirer was born into the kingdom of Jesus Christ. God's power had ripped another hole in the dark canopy over Bako!"[5] Since prayer journeyers have been going to this once-resistant area, 1,100 believers have come to know the Lord!

Throughout the 10/40 Window, stories abound showing how God's greater power triumphs in the midst of darkness. Bryant Myers, in the December 1996 MARC newsletter, testifies to the power of God to transform lives in India: "A house made of cardboard was where [a poverty-stricken woman] and her husband lived in Madras [now Chennai]. During every monsoon the flimsy structure would wash away in the flooding tides. They were among the poorest of the poor. Work was irregular for the couple. With no steady income, they couldn't afford the expensive bricks they needed to build a sturdier, more permanent dwelling. When the husband did get work as a day laborer, he used the money to buy liquor. They have a better life now because they met the Savior. 'We lived on the little I could earn. But when we became Christians, my husband stopped drinking,' she reported with a bright light in her eyes. 'We decided that, since we already knew how to survive on what I earned, we would save what my husband earned until there was enough to buy five bricks. Then we would improve our home five bricks at a time. This is how Jesus has changed our lives.'"

A prayer journeyer from a church in Woodland Park, Colorado, submitted a report dated 13 April 1998 about a prayer journey the previous year: "During my prayer journey to Myanmar, a 75-year-old Rawang church planter named Tychicus told me one example of government interference. In the Rakhine state there is a lot of resistance to the Gospel. In 1996 the government there sent a group of soldiers to a church in a village named Lanmadaw to dismantle it board-by-bamboo-pole!

"As the soldiers began the dismantling process, the Buddhist monks there scoffed at the God of the Christians, saying that He could do nothing to stop them, and that their own god was more powerful than that of the Christians. At that moment a great darkness fell over Lanmadaw as black clouds formed. Then lightning bolts came from the clouds and struck the local Buddhist temple, a very sacred place in that area and home to these boasting Buddhist monks. Fifteen lightning bolts struck the temple and left it in slivers. Each bolt cut a crevice clear through the temple so that one could look in from one end and out of the other end. Fifteen such slices through the structure left it in shambles!"

The prayer report goes on to say that the son of the village leader who had masterminded the dismantling of the Christian church suddenly fell dead for no apparent reason. In addition, 35 Buddhist devotees journeying towards Lanmadaw to worship at this temple were killed when their boat mysteriously struck a much larger craft. Because of these sobering events, Christian churches in the region now have a greater level of safety.

The February 1998 *Sikkim Winter Trekking Report* gave several encouraging accounts of the Holy Spirit's work in the Indian state of Sikkim:

"During a showing of the *JESUS* film, teams of Christian workers experienced resistance in some of the places they were doing evangelistic work. Tracts were burned, and attempts were made to damage the film equipment. One evangelist was dragged into a village home and beaten. The instigator of this attack later accepted the Lord, repented of his actions, and asked forgiveness from the evangelist."

The report from Sikkim also shares this story: "One team was urgently warned not to go to a certain area as they would be beaten and perhaps killed, but after prayer they were convinced they should continue. God opened the way for them, and they were well received. The villagers asked for a team to come and teach them and establish a church. This happened in several places."

Also in Sikkim, "healings occur in many villages as teams of evangelists continue to preach the Good News. One man, paralyzed for some time, was healed. The villagers had never seen such a thing, were astonished, and fell to the ground on their knees praising the Lord. The team was given food and shelter and the villagers begged them to 'come back and start a church.' They were often given gifts of food and told, 'No one has ever come to us with this news before,' or, 'We never heard of this Jesus before.'"

The people of Saudi Arabia are virtually unreached by the Gospel. God, however, has unique and creative ways to reach people with the Good News. A number of reports tell of Saudis having dreams and visions in which they see Jesus. They then seek out Christians to find out what the dreams mean and subsequently come to salvation. Some out of curiosity are listening to Christian radio broadcasts and then turning to Jesus Christ as their Savior.

However, those who become believers live in grave danger. Saudi Arabia is an Islamic kingdom committed to the preservation of traditional Islam. Anyone converting from Islam to another religion risks capital punishment. In 1992 a Saudi Muslim was beheaded because he became a believer in Christ. Apostate Muslims are often poisoned. Because of this persecution, new believers are reluctant to start churches because it might cost them their lives.

Still, strategies are being developed to reach the Saudis. Even in Saudi Arabia, a stronghold of traditional Islam, the Gospel of Jesus Christ is not chained (2 Tim. 2:9).

Breakthroughs in Receptivity

Several other countries historically resistant to Christian witness have shown promising signs of receptivity in recent years.

The Spring 1998 *10/40 Window Reporter* tells how Pastor/ Evangelist Benny Hinn met with Jordan's King Hussein. This all came about when Pastor Hinn invited Jordan's Minister of Tourism to his Nashville outreach, during which Pastor Hinn urged Christians to pray for and support the country of Jordan. The Jordanian official passed along the video of this event to King Hussein's eldest son, Prince Abdullah, and the prince then gave it to his father. Shortly afterwards, Pastor Hinn was invited to meet with the king. He used the opportunity to share his desire to bring Christian leaders from America to meet him. King Hussein was in favor of the idea.

During the summer of 1998, Pastor Hinn returned to Jordan with 1,050 Christians to tour the country at the king's invitation. What an amazing turn of events. A Jordanian believer reported that local newspapers covered the story with accounts of how "the king had invited 1,000 Christian pilgrims to Jordan." Can you imagine—the king called the Christians to be guests of this Muslim country!

On the evening Pastor Hinn's meetings began, the Minister of Tourism welcomed the Americans and said, "Thank you for accepting the king's invitation." Then he read from the Bible that Jesus was baptized in the Jordan River by John the Baptist, and that while Jesus was being baptized God spoke from heaven and declared, "This is My beloved Son, in whom I am well pleased" (Matt. 3:17).

A Jordanian believer writes, "This was a nice miracle, but the biggest miracle was that some people from Jordan accepted the Lord!" Jesus was lifted high that night.[6]

Another good report originates from HCJB World Radio about new openness in Cambodia: "From a land that once was extremely hostile to Christianity comes remarkable news. Two engineers traveled to Phnom Penh in March 1998 to install a transmitter for the first Christian radio station in the country. The government of Cambodia gave HCJB World Radio permission to put a 'suitcase' radio station on the air. God persuaded the government officials to grant permission for this project."

In India, thousands of lives were touched after God delivered a man from mental illness. Evangelist Dale Sexauer sends this account: "The mentally ill man was known throughout the town of Firozpur, in the Punjab state on India's border with Pakistan. His illness was so severe that he had been kept on a chain like a wild animal for the past eight years. Then, during an evangelistic event at the end of April 1997, the cheering crowd could hardly control its excitement as they saw the man walk onto the stage without his chain, which an assistant was carrying. Jesus Christ became the talk of the town.

"Around 50,000 people attended the last event of the 18-day mission. Weeks after the meetings ended, hundreds of people were still waiting to be baptized. Sexauer reported that more than 1,000 people experienced some form of healing or deliverance. It is just like Jesus to free the demon-possessed and to heal the many diseases of humankind. He provides the breakthrough. People in the surrounding villages have opened to the Gospel after hearing reports of healings."

Faith under Fire and God's Deliverance

The Everlasting Lord reigns. He is actively seeking out people to redeem and bring into His everlasting kingdom. Here is a testimony from India of God's love and grace that will bring the reality of the Good News into focus. R. Vasudeva Rao writes, "At 19 I was a dangerous character. I blindly followed the Hindu religious rituals, customs, and practices in my younger days, but I craved something that would satisfy my innermost being. Failure to find peace in my heart made me a menace to society. My father asked me to leave home.

"Eventually, I decided to end my life. As I walked down a busy road, I found an India Every Home for Christ (EHC) Gospel booklet lying on the sidewalk. I read the booklet over and over. Never in my life had I heard that God sent Jesus to die for my sins.

"I decided to take this opportunity to get myself right and wrote to the India Every Home for Christ office at Bangalore for the Bible correspondence course. As I studied the lessons, I became convinced that Jesus Christ is the Son of God and trusted Him for my salvation.

"The people in my village observed a difference in me. I became an entirely changed man. I kept busy reading the follow-up books, Bible lessons, and New Testament sent from the EHC office. I told my parents about Jesus, the true God. My father shouted at me, and my mother was unhappy that her son would leave the ancestral gods and embrace Christianity.

"My parents tried every method to bring me around. Seeing that I was adamant, they didn't mind losing me rather than allowing me to join that 'wretched religion.' So my parents hired a killer to follow me into the woods where I regularly went in the evenings for prayer.

"As I was praying in the woods, the hired man came near with a heavy club; but seeing me kneeling and praying, he couldn't understand why he was asked to hurt a man who was so godly. He left without harming me.

"I received counseling and further instruction from the India Every Home for Christ office and was eventually asked to join the EHC staff. I gladly accepted the offer and joined the follow-up department. I write letters to Hindus, helping them know Jesus Christ as their Savior and grow in their faith."[7]

Two more stories from India illustrate how God rescues the lost from lives of despair and bondage to the powers of the evil one:

Their eyes heavy from lack of sleep, a police officer and his family lived in constant terror as powers of darkness consumed their lives. Haunted by dreadful figures strangling him at night, the officer in Karnataka state found no rest until he met a national missionary who, led by God, brought him the saving message of Jesus. Brother K. V. Jayavel shared the redemption of Christ with the police officer while doing pioneer work—street witnessing in villages, holding home prayer fellowships, and visiting hospitals—in remote areas of the state. Though the officer had been a devout orthodox Hindu from his youth, he had no peace of mind. As Brother Jayavel shared the Gospel with him, the officer gave his life to Jesus. The new believer invited Jayavel to his house to pray.

"Claiming the promises of God, I asked the Lord to cover the home with the precious Blood of Jesus and set them free from the powers of darkness," said Jayavel. The Lord was faithful to replace the darkness with His eternal peace and joy. No one in the family experienced any more troubles at night. The whole family was overwhelmed with Christ's awesome love. They gave up their idol worship and received Jesus. Now they share their testimony with the villagers. In addition, Jayavel was deeply encouraged to persevere in his ministry. Within six months Brother Jayavel saw 25 people commit their lives to the Lord and be baptized, as God works mightily through him.[8]

God does everything perfectly, working in truly marvelous ways according to His perfect plan as the following story illustrates. Three students from a Bible school in Bangalore, India, were doing outreach work. They prayed and asked the Lord to lead them to the right person with whom they could share the Gospel. They were led to go out to the railway line near a certain village, where they saw a couple by the tracks. As a train came towards the couple, the woman unsuccessfully attempted to force her companion away from the tracks. The students succeeded in pulling the man to safety before the oncoming train reached them.

The man was sobbing uncontrollably. Through his tears, he conveyed his story to the students. He said that he was troubled with life and could not find happiness or satisfaction. He was despondent about his life's problems and had decided to finish his life that evening by throwing himself under the train.

The men listened patiently for him to finish his story, then explained that the Lord had sent them there with a specific purpose. They told him that they had had no plans to come near the railway track that evening but had felt led to go there. They clearly explained to the man and his wife the plan of salvation. Both of them listened intently. They could not imagine that God loved them so much that He had sent these three brothers to save the husband's life. The husband and wife began to understand the love of God for them when they heard He sent His Son, Jesus Christ, to die on the cross for their sins.

It seemed impossible for them to fully comprehend the extent to which the Lord loved and cared for them. With tears streaming down their cheeks, they both gave their hearts to the Lord.[9]

Harvest Amidst Crisis

A May 1998 report from Asia identifies several ways in which the Holy Spirit is working in the midst of difficult circumstances to advance the kingdom of God.

Out of the political and economic chaos in Asia, God is bringing His plan to pass. Though Satan may try to use Asia's troubles for his purposes, the believers there are taking advantage of the turmoil to spread the Gospel. Asian churches believe this is now the time for harvest. Often people are more receptive to the Gospel during a crisis. Here are some methods the Church in Asia is using to reach the lost:

- Churches of like mind are networking to carry the Gospel to other nations.
- Cell churches are sending entire cells to the mission field on short-term mission trips.
- There is an emerging long-term mission commitment; career missions are just now catching on like wildfire.
- New models of business are emerging out of Asia and being used as an avenue for missions.
- God is also using more power evangelism, spiritual warfare, prayer strategies, inner-city ministries, and outreach to drug addicts and recovered drug addicts, prostitutes, inner city gangs, AIDS patients, runaways and unwed mothers as avenues for church planting.
- There is an emphasis on country-specific and people-specific training for missionaries.
- A greater team missions concept is emerging with less emphasis on individual involvement on the mission field and more on partnering with other believers in the task of getting the Gospel to every nation.
- There is a resurgence of tentmaking in order to enter countries historically closed to missions activities.

Unity in Prayer Is the Key to Pulling Down Strongholds

Since 1993, the *Praying Through The Window* initiatives have mobilized the prayers of millions of believers across the globe for the 10/40 Window, and we can now see that the exponential power of God released by these prayers is having a profound effect within the Window. Although all too often underutilized by believers, the magnificent power of prayer is a mighty weapon from the Lord. By exercising our authority on the earth in prayer on behalf of those precious souls for whom Jesus Christ died, we are seeing the Lord triumph in the 10/40 Window daily.

In some places where missionaries previously reported few salvation decisions, the Church is now experiencing phenomenal growth. Some evangelistic agencies report that house churches in China add tens of thousands of new believers to their congregations monthly. Our prayers have an impact.

Youth With A Mission and many other groups sponsor a prayer focus for the nearly 100 million Arabs who celebrate the month of Ramadan. During Ramadan, devout Muslims fast from dawn to sunset for 30 days. Pray that these seekers of God would find salvation through our Lord Jesus Christ.

An example of God's power working through the united prayers of believers comes from John Robb of MARC (a division of World Vision International). In March 1998 he reported that a recent prayer initiative in Ethiopia brought together more than 150 churches and prayer leaders for a three-day prayer conference. The prayer focused on Ethiopia, Sudan, Somalia, Eritrea, and Djibouti. Presentations were made on intercession, stewardship, redemption of the nation for Christ, and spiritual warfare. Between the presentations, there were intense times of intercession. Many of the prayer sessions focused on unreached people groups, the war in Sudan, the rebuilding of the national government in Somalia, social and economic problems in Djibouti, and the current flight ban hindering humanitarian aid.

On one particular prayer journey in Ethiopia, team members received two troubling visions concerning the bloodguilt affecting Ethiopia's land and churches. The team accompanied several local leaders to an area near Addis Ababa, the nation's capital, where the former emperor Haile Selassie and the Marxist dictator Mengistu Haile Mariam are said to have carried out frequent human sacrifices to spiritual powers in their thirst to maintain power and control. The Ethiopian Christians repented of the sins of idolatry and bloodshed on behalf of their forefathers and rulers and renounced agreements that were made with demonic powers. The believers expressed that they had a noticeable sense of cleansing and renewal after the time of repentance. Everyone took the Lord's Supper at this location, affirming the power of Jesus' Blood to absorb all the defilement that penetrated the land.

Christians believe that the prayer of repentance initiates a powerful weapon of our warfare. In May 1998 in Galveston, Texas, I (Beverly) received a vision vividly illustrating that we have ultimate victory over the power of darkness:

"This morning I was praying about the medical work of Dr. Raju Abraham, a prominent Christian doctor in India. The Lord showed me that there is an all-out battle in the spiritual realm for the souls of the people in India. As the saints of God are praying for this region, the Lord is responding to our prayers by dispatching a powerful army of warring angels. I saw this fierce battle. As we prayed, the army of angels grew larger and stronger and began destroying the powers of darkness."

As children of God we enjoy the assurance that God ultimately triumphs over evil. Yet until that day, the war against Satan's forces rages on. We must continue to wield our heavenly weapons in order to see the devil's defeat on this earth. We cannot let up. We must stay fervent in prayer. The weapons of our warfare are not carnal, but they are mighty through God for the pulling down of demonic structures (2 Cor. 10:4). We must persevere in prayer. Commitment to disciplined prayer and action is the mandate of the hour. Through the prayers of believers and unity in the Body of Christ, the world will see that our God *is* greater than the powers of darkness.

You Can Help Meet the Challenge

- Stay informed. Read newspapers and magazines, taking note of trouble spots around the world, and pray.
- Start a notebook in which you jot down pertinent information about crises, famines, earthquakes, droughts, armed conflicts, etc.
- Subscribe to Christian publications that are at the forefront of reaching the lost in unevangelized or underevangelized countries.

- Covenant with God to consecrate one hour each week to pray for the nations in the 10/40 Window.
- Fast at least one meal per week. Send the cost of that meal to ministries actively involved in missions work outside your country.
- Inform your local church fellowship about persecuted Christians around the world. Gather a group of dedicated prayer warriors who will intercede on behalf of the suffering Church in other nations.
- Reach out to people from other cultures who live in your city and share the Good News of Jesus Christ.
- Meet with other believers outside your ethnic group, denomination, or fellowship, to break down barriers and build bridges.

Endnotes

1. Source: Ray G. Register, Jr., *Back to Jerusalem: Church Planting in the Holy Land,* Baptist Village 45875, Israel, 1997, page 9 (unpublished manuscript)
2. Source: Lynn Green, "Under Way! The Reconciliation Walk Sets Off from Cologne, Germany," *Prayer Track News,* Vol. 5, No. 3, July–October 1996, pp. 4–5
3. Source: "Christians Retrace Crusader's Steps," *Christianity Today,* October 7, 1996, p.36 by Rusty Wright
4. Source: "Frontline News," *The 10/40 Window Reporter,* Vol. 2, No. 2, Spring 1998, p. 9
5. Bob Havenor, *Alliance Life,* 12 February 1997, p. 26
6. Source: *10/40 Window Reporter,* Vol. 2 No. 2, Spring 1998, p. 9
7. Source: R. Vasudeva Rao, Every Home for Christ, reported by Brigada 17 April 1997
8. Source: Gospel For Asia, report posted on their web site 8 April 1997
9. Source: India For Christ Ministries, Madanapalle Mission Field, Andhra Pradesh

4

Disarming the Powers of Darkness

*T*hirteen-year-old Lakshmi held the bottle of pesticide to her lips and prepared to die. If life offered nothing better than her experiences so far, suicide was the preferable option.

Born into extreme poverty in Bangalore, India, Lakshmi had begun a slow descent into living hell after her father died. Lakshmi's mother compelled her and her sister to beg for food and scavenge for rags to earn a few coins for the family. Then, after her mother remarried, Lakshmi's stepfather tried to rape her. The girl ran away to her grandmother's home, but heartaches awaited her there, too.

Her grandmother ran a brothel of young girls forced into prostitution to earn money. Ill-treated and sexually abused, Lakshmi escaped to the streets and once again scrounged for rags to sell. Without any hope for shelter, security, or love, she despaired of life one day and tried to poison herself.

Other rag-pickers she had met on the street grabbed the pesticide bottle and threw it away, rescuing her. Then a miracle occurred. A social worker found the dark-eyed Hindu girl and brought her to the Grace Destitute Home, a world apart from any she had ever known. Lakshmi marveled to learn that the Home, sponsored by the Grace Gospel Mission, offered food, shelter, and even job skills training to young girls like her.

With a program ministering to physical, emotional, and spiritual needs, Grace Gospel Mission incorporates a dynamic ministry of prayer for the sick and demon possessed with vigorous evangelism. Since the project's inception in 1985, close to 5,000 people, most of them from a Hindu background, have given their hearts to Jesus and been baptized.

Two keys to this ministry, in addition to its combination of sign, word, and deed on its own premises, are the 24-hour prayer chain operated by the church and the availability at all times of the pastor and his staff to minister to local slum dwellers and other sick and needy people. Even state authorities have recognized and commended the Bangalore outreach for its effective service to the poor.

Thanks to the Grace Destitute Home, Lakshmi can now read and write. In the past five years, she also has learned to stitch, knit, and make handicraft items. Life at the Home fills her daily with joy. But the best benefit is eternal. Lakshmi has accepted Jesus Christ as her Savior and has been baptized.

Ministering to Body, Soul, and Spirit

How can the Church conquer the powers of darkness, minister to the needs of the poor, speak against oppression, and point toward Jesus those who are perishing? We find our clues by studying the life of Jesus. Our Lord cared for all aspects of the tripartite human nature—body, soul, and spirit. When we model our lives and ministries after Jesus, we will find the Church of Jesus Christ wielding incredible influence in a fallen world. As we preach the Gospel, we should also act as a voice for the poor, the powerless, and the persecuted, partnering with them to help find means of meeting their needs. "Faith without deeds is dead" (James 2:26).

Out of compassion, Jesus fed the multitudes, preached the Word of God, raised the dead, healed the sick, and drove out tormenting evil spirits. He ministered to people's needs on every level and challenged and defeated the demonic power structure holding them in bondage (Col. 2:15).

Eight times Scripture mentions that Jesus had compassion on people. The Greek word *splanchnizomai* means to have the bowels yearn, i.e. to feel inward affection, sympathy, or pity, to be moved with compassion, to have one's heart go out to others. Jesus' tenderness and empathy toward others motivated His ministry because these are characteristics of God the Father. In John 4:34, Jesus said, "My food is to do the will of him who sent me and to finish his work." Christ on earth fulfilled everything that was written about Him in the Law of Moses, the Prophets, and the Psalms (Luke 24:44). As we model our ministry after the compassion of Jesus, let us determine to do the will of Him who sent us and to finish His agenda, not our own.

Commissioned with Authority

Jesus' intention was to pass on His work to His disciples. He carefully selected the original 12 after praying all night (Luke 6:12-13). He trained them in His philosophy, leadership style, and approach to ministry. He prepared them for effective service, then sent them out to minister to the needs of the people. Later Jesus trained and commissioned 72 more. The disciples returned from their mission rejoicing that the demons submitted to them in His Name. Jesus reminded His disciples that He was the one who gave them authority to trample on snakes and overcome all the power of the enemy. He kept them focused and told them to rejoice that their names were written in the Lamb's Book of Life (Luke 10:17-20).

God's Word says clearly that He has already given the Church authority to overpower all demonic forces on earth (Luke 10:19; 2 Cor. 5:18-20, 10:4-5). We have the responsibility, therefore, to watch over the spiritual condition of nations and to overcome all evil principalities on behalf of those under their influence. We must make the world aware of the atrocities of religious persecution and use our influence to see it end. We also have an obligation to seek God for ways to provide for the poor, to conquer disease and malnutrition, to foster literacy, and to liberate the oppressed.

From the beginning, God gave human beings the awesome responsibility of ruling and reigning over the earth. God holds sovereign authority, but He has delegated dominion over the earth to us (Gen. 1:28). Exercising our God-given authority on the earth will keep many people from spending eternity in hell.

We have been given authority in order to fulfill a God-given mandate. "Therefore go and make disciples of all nations, baptizing them in the name of the Father and of the Son and of the Holy Spirit, and teaching them to obey everything I have commanded you. And surely I am with you always, to the very end of the age" (Matt. 28:19-20). Our mandate, simply stated, is to take the Gospel to all people groups, make disciples, and baptize them and teach them to obey the Word of God.

Humankind has turned over the government of the earth to ungodly leaders and cruel governing bodies that are influenced by demonic power structures. Yet God's command to rule and reign still holds, and He would not give us this charge without empowering us to fulfill it.

We, the Church, have the only answer for a world full of idolatry, hate, violence, and destruction—Jesus Christ. The Gospel of Christ will transform humanity and thereby transition societies from the kingdom of darkness to the kingdom of light. God gave us the command to take His glorious Gospel to the ends of the earth, because He fully knew how desperate the condition of the nations today would be. The Good News will rescue humankind from godlessness and guarantee freedom and eternal life in Jesus Christ. He is the only answer for the world. There is no other.

The Power of God's Love

The 10/40 Window nations, however, know little or nothing about the freedom and peace Jesus Christ brings. These nations are ruled by the strongman of fear. People groups there serve demonic deities because they are afraid of the demons' power.

Most believe that these demons are their only source of blessing and prosperity, and that if they do not appease the evil spirits they will suffer. Why do they think this way? In their cultures, demonic power is real and present in a way that is almost inconceivable to a Western mindset.

Those whose home is the 10/40 Window have grown up experiencing firsthand the manifestation of powerful demonic principalities who rule their villages and surrounding areas. Most of those who live in the grip of fear consider their way of life normal and believe that everyone suffers in dread of demonic deities. They have never experienced the love of God and don't know that our King wields power far beyond that of any evil spirits. When they hear for the first time that there is a God who loves them and wants a relationship with them, many respond by devoting their lives to Him.

A church in Cleveland, Tennessee, had been praying for the Mahotari Tharu people of Nepal for two years. Over the months the church members had come to feel God's heart of love for these lost souls so precious to Him. In January 1997, the church decided to send a small scouting prayer team to Nepal to make contact with their unreached people group. They arranged with acquaintances in Kathmandu to join English/Nepali interpreters and travel to the region near where the Mahotari Tharus live.

After 12 days in the country, the team had not located the remote Tharu villages, and only two days remained before they had to return home. On the day before their departure, they found an 11-year-old Tharu boy who said he could direct the team to his people. However, the Tharus' homeland lay quite a distance away in this mountainous country, and the prayer team did not have time to trek there and back before boarding their plane. The team left disappointed. They knew their church, too, would grieve that they had been unable to reach their beloved Tharus.

Four months later, after more prayer, the church sensed the Holy Spirit wanted them to return to Nepal to seek the unreached people they had come to love through prayer. This time the senior pastor from the church joined the prayer team. Before and throughout their journey, they prayed that the Holy Spirit would lead them to the young boy who could tell the team's translators how to find the Mahotari Tharus.

Only God could arrange this—and He did! The team found the boy on the eighth day of their return trip. The youngster gave directions to the team and translators, who then made contact with a leprosy hospital in the area to pinpoint the location of the Tharu villages. The translators cautioned the team that tribes in that region had a reputation for violent opposition to outsiders preaching the Gospel. Fearing that trouble could start, the translators told the rest of the team, "If we run, you run!" The prayer journeyers knew the Holy Spirit was directing them to take the love and truth of Christ to the Tharus they held so dear, so they were willing to risk their lives to do it.

Traveling through dry riverbeds and over oxcart trails, the team and translators eventually arrived in the isolated Tharu homeland. They asked to meet with the chief. The pastor gave a typical Western greeting and explained why they were there. "We come from America," he said, "and we would like to know more about you and your people." At this point, the chief was formal yet cordial. Then the pastor's love and compassion gushed forth, and he confessed, "Our church has prayed for you for two years, and we've come to get to know you."

The chief took the pastor by the hand, a Tharu custom for people with whom they bond, and personally showed the prayer team around the village. The chief also gave the prayer team permission to show a Nepali translation of the *JESUS* film depicting the life of Jesus through the words of the Gospel of Luke.

The Tharus in this village had never heard about Jesus the Savior. The manifest expression of God's love, through both the film and the living example of the team who had come so far to meet them, melted their hearts. After the team's return to the States, the pastor, with tears brimming in his eyes, exclaimed to his church, "Five Tharus gave their lives to Jesus after watching the *JESUS* film in their own language!" He went on, "All of my life I wanted to lead someone to the Lord who had never heard the Gospel." God granted him that privilege during this prayer journey by allowing him to visit the people for whom he and his church had interceded. Two years before the prayer journey, when the church prayed that the Gospel would penetrate the Tharus' darkness, they did not know that they would be the answer to their own prayers. These believers planted a church among the Tharu people in Nepal in November 1998. Fueled by compassion, this local church put feet to their prayers.[1]

Love in Action

Many unreached peoples don't have a word for love in their vocabulary. Bound by fear of demonic spirits, they often find it difficult to understand a loving God. It is our responsibility, therefore, to demonstrate the love of Jesus Christ to them through the example of our lifestyle. When they see in our actions the nature and power of love, they will long for this in their own lives. God loved the world so much that He sent Jesus, His one and only Son, to build a bridge across the chasm of sin and redeem humanity to Himself. When our hearts are filled with love for the lost, we too will be ready to sacrifice to show them God's love.

An Armenian couple who co-pastors a church in Amman, Jordan, told us a story about their seven-year-old son, Aren. On New Year's Eve 1997, they invited the security guard in their building to come to their annual celebration at the church. Sami, an Egyptian from a nominal Christian background, accepted the invitation.

Aren sat beside Sami during the church service, helping him find that evening's worship songs. When time came for communion, Sami didn't partake because he felt unworthy. Aren observed this, and his heart sank. He saw this as a sure sign that Sami didn't have a personal relationship with Jesus Christ. As the service ended, Aren ran to his mother, crying uncontrollably. "Mom, Sami is going to hell!" he sobbed.

Surprised, his mother asked, "Why?" Aren told her that Sami didn't take communion. Aren's mom comforted him by asking one of the male soul winners to share the Gospel with Sami. This man sat with Sami and Aren explaining the Good News until the guard gave his life to Jesus.

Now Sami comes to church every Sunday and always brings his friends, many of whom have also accepted the Lord. Because God poured His love and compassion for Sami into Aren, the guard was able to relate to the love of Christ through his young friend. Sami was amazed that Aren could love him so much that he would weep over his lost soul. What a powerful illustration of the love of God flowing through a seven-year-old boy!

Prayer Empowers Ministry to the Whole Person

No ministry can be sustained without prayer. Neither acts of love nor witnessing—if done in human power alone—will bring lasting transformation. To fulfill our mandate, we must receive empowerment from Almighty God. Prayer enables us to draw on and release that power in service to those who need God's light to shine in their darkness.

John Robb of World Vision's MARC writes,[2] "Through Christ's redemption, human stewardship over the earth is being restored. And through prayer, we as His redeemed people reassert our God-given dominion over the world, ruling and reigning with Christ. Through believing prayer, we open the door for God's intervention in our troubled world, and open ourselves up to become part of God's answer to that world of need."

John's article, written with Larry Wilson and entitled "In God's Kingdom…Prayer Is Social Action," shows how prayer is the indispensable link between effective evangelism and compassionate concern for social needs. "After 11 years of combining evangelism and economic development among the world's poor through World Vision," John says, "I can say there is no holistic transformation of people apart from united intercession by God's people."

Why is prayer so important? "United prayer," John declares, "weakens and pushes back the spiritual darkness blinding countries, towns, and individuals, enabling them to hear and see the Good News of Jesus Christ. United prayer opens hearts to a new way of living, and when hearts are changed, so are the communities in which people live."

Do we really believe that God cares about a suffering world? Do we believe God will intervene in the affairs of humankind? If so, we must call on Him and His power to fulfill every endeavor He calls us to undertake.

The 1998 Kumbh Mela Outreach

The following story, forwarded to us by a reliable source in an e-mail message of 7 June 1998, shows the importance of prayer combined with compassion and the benefits of working in strategic partnership. No other means could have produced such phenomenal results.

"The Kumbh Mela, an important Hindu festival celebrated in India every three years in rotation between the four 'holy' cities of Allahabad, Haridwar, Ujjain and Nasik, is possibly the largest periodic gathering of humanity anywhere in the world.

"The 1998 Kumbh Mela took place at Haridwar, in Uttar Pradesh, from January through mid-May. Haridwar is situated in the foothills of the Himalayas, where the Ganges River begins its journey to the plains below. The most revered site in Haridwar is Har-ki-Pauri, a concrete *ghat* or embankment of steps constructed along the Ganges for ritual bathing. Hindu *sadhus* (holy men) and pilgrims converge upon Har-ki-Pauri during the Kumbh Mela, in the hope of having their sins washed away by the sacred river. They also pray they might be blessed by the gods in this life and the next, and escape the endless cycle of reincarnation by attaining salvation. This year's Kumbh Mela was considered especially significant as the last of the millennium.

"After viewing a British Broadcasting Company documentary on the 1989 Allahabad Kumbh Mela, we realized that the major key to achieving a spiritual breakthrough is prayer and intercession. We began to mobilize international prayer for the 1998 Mela at Haridwar.

"In response to prayer, the Holy Spirit brought us into contact with other ministries and leaders with the same burden for

India, many of whom were already planning pre-Mela prayer activities. In mid-1997, several teams relocated to Uttar Pradesh to begin networking with others in the area.

"God gave us a two-fold strategy for equipping and mobilizing hundreds of believers for outreach to the Haridwar Mela. The dual thrusts of this strategy were prayer and outreach/literature distribution.

"Several prayer events were organized before and during the Kumbh Mela, starting a year in advance. These included early morning corporate intercession, monthly prayer journeys to cover the five main highways leading into Haridwar, regular fasting with prayer, monthly 24-hour prayer and worship sessions that increased in frequency during the Mela to include each high bathing day, international prayer that continued after the festival through use of a 30-day prayer guide, and an extended time of prayer and worship on Easter weekend, 10–12 April 1998.

"In addition to prayer, the two-fold strategy included outreach and literature distribution. We had tracts designed specifically for distribution during the Mela, both for the common person and for the intellectual. Two million were printed in Hindi and thousands in other Indian languages.

"We designated railway and bus stations along the major routes into Haridwar as the main sites for tract distribution, and 30 key neighboring cities as centers for outreach. More than 600 young people, strategically placed into 65 teams, participated in these efforts during April and May 1998.

"The Lord gave us many answers to prayer, both for the Body of Christ and for unbelievers:

"*Unprecedented Unity:* In the early days of prayer and preparation, the Holy Spirit impressed upon us that unity would be key to seeing substantial fruitfulness. As we made this a major focus of prayer, the unity that developed among the international, national, and local organizations was amazing. Some gave substantial amounts of money; others mobilized outreach teams to send to neighboring cities.

"*Worship Conference:* With prayer and worship our main strategy, we felt the need to kick off the outreach by preparing our own hearts before giving out. A 29-member ministry team from the United Kingdom led a three-day worship conference. The Holy Spirit revealed that as the Body of Christ worshiped in spirit and in truth, giving devotion to the one true and living God, we would push back the powers of darkness and India would fulfill her God-given destiny and redemptive purpose. We also received insight that indigenous worship and worship leaders must be encouraged and developed.

"*The Jesus March:* Some 150 believers took part in a 'Jesus March' through the streets of Haridwar from 4 to 7 a.m. on Easter Sunday, two days before the final high bathing day of the Mela. In an inexplicable miracle, local authorities granted permission for the March; then, within a few hours after the March's completion, a surprise ban was issued on all remaining processions for the rest of the festival, even those of the sadhus! Haridwar's first-ever Jesus March broke through a spiritual stronghold of fear among local believers.

"*Low Turnout of Pilgrims:* The organizers of the festival had expected between 10 and 20 million pilgrims. To their great disappointment, only a fraction of that number actually came, perhaps 4 million total over the four-month period. Opening day of the festival proved a particular disaster; 400,000 pilgrims were expected, but only an estimated 4,000 showed up! Because of the low turnout, the Mela was a financial catastrophe.

"We asked the Lord to discourage pilgrims from making the journey at all, and to create an honest question in people's hearts as to why they should dip in a river to have their sins washed away. The Holy Spirit allowed several factors to work together to see this prayer realized. Political uncertainty before and after the general elections, held from mid-February through early March, made people afraid of traveling, as unrest haunts the nation during elections. Other factors included unusually bad weather, with the first of several high bathing days experiencing heavy downpours, a rumored bomb attack by militants, and reports of sadhu groups clashing with police.

"*Chaos in the Camp:* On the night before the high bathing day of Chitra Amavasya (28 March), sadhus from two rival factions disagreed about which of them should first take the "holy dip." The argument turned violent the next day, and police had to step in to restore order. The irate sadhus, however, attacked the officers and began throwing stones and burning vehicles. About 45 sadhus and seven police officers were hospitalized, and authorities deployed a special armed police force to monitor the situation. Barricades were set up at significant points in the city, creating inconvenient diversions for pilgrims who then had to walk long distances to reach Har-ki-Pauri. The whole incident further discouraged pilgrims from attending the rest of the Mela.

"*Openness to the Gospel:* As the Mela progressed, we saw a growing openness to the Gospel in the hearts of people from various walks of life.

- Literature distribution led to conversations with thousands of pilgrims. The results were very encouraging, with unprecedented receptivity to the Good News.
- An important police official asked some local believers to share their message at a gathering of 200 police officers.
- During several prayer times, we felt led to focus on praying specifically for the sadhus, since these men hold a place of great influence over the pilgrims, and once saved can have tremendous impact for the kingdom of God. Within a few weeks after the Kumbh Mela outreach, several sadhus had come to faith in Christ.
- A 25-year-old sadhu heard the Gospel for the first time from one of our teams on the second-highest day of the Mela. The Good News so pierced his heart that he went home, washed and shaved his dreadlocks and beard— symbols of his status as a sadhu—even before returning to the team and making a profession of faith! He soon accepted Jesus as his Lord and Savior. He remained with us for the duration of the outreach, participating in worship times and speaking enthusiastically about his new-birth experience. He is now being discipled by one of our teams and blossoming in his faith.
- Two other sadhus wandered into the church compound after arriving in the city by train. They were greeted by some Christians with breakfast and water to wash. So

overwhelmed were they by the kindness and respect shown to them by our team that they decided to bypass the ritual bathing in the Ganges, the very reason for their trip to Haridwar!

- Another sadhu had contact with our team members. They explained the Gospel to him over a period of several days, his first encounter with the Good News. A few days later, while he was performing his religious rites in a Hindu temple, the Holy Spirit came upon him and he started confessing Jesus as Lord. He had experienced tremendous pain in his shoulder and decided to pray for healing in Jesus' Name. God touched his body and healed him! Two days later he returned to meet with our workers and dedicated his life to the Lord Jesus, whom he had just met in a powerful way.

"Throughout the outreach, we encountered a minimum of resistance and no real persecution. God had prepared the way for the teams to find receptive hearts in people wanting to know more."[3]

Disarming Demonic Powers

The story from our source about the Kumbh Mela outreach gives clear illustration of the importance of prayer in disarming the powers of darkness. Only through prayer could the team receive God's strategy for the outreach. Their intercession released the power of the Holy Spirit to advance the kingdom of God. Prayer kept them in communication with the Lord and in fellowship with each other.

John Robb explains why dependence on God's power through prayer is crucial for success in our commission. "Since the garden of Eden, humans have cooperated with Satan and his evil spirits to gain control over individuals and societies, leading to widescale famine, disease, poverty, slavery, injustice, and suffering. Whenever we try to help the victims of these tragedies, we enter a fray involving the great socio-spiritual forces that rule the world's massive institutions, social structures, and systems."[4]

A ministry that combines prayer, evangelism, and social action has tremendous potential because of its ability to disarm these demonic forces. When we address the problems of society in the Name of Jesus and the power of the Holy Spirit, we dismantle the footholds of evil that give ground to the enemy.

Engaging in spiritual warfare through ministry to the spirit, soul, and body is part of the commission of the Body of Christ because many governments in the 10/40 Window rule in tyranny. These rulers are held captive by demonic power systems. Many have no respect for the value of their citizens' lives. Slavery persists in a number of Window countries, and many inhumane acts of violence against women and children are reported from this part of the world. Not coincidentally, these areas also exhibit the most resistance to the Gospel message and persecute Christians vigorously.

The Church has a responsibility to speak on behalf of the suffering and oppressed of these countries. Even secular structures such as the United Nations can bring pressure on governments to reform unjust practices. Sixty-one countries of the 10/40 Window belong to the United Nations, whose Universal Declaration of Human Rights (December 1948) states in its preamble, "Member States have pledged themselves to achieve, in cooperation with the United Nations, the promotion of universal respect for and observance of human rights and fundamental freedoms." The Church can have even greater impact than secular organizations because we know that the root cause of tyranny is bondage to demonic forces, and only the Body of Christ is equipped to disarm these evil powers.

Prayer remains the key to effective ministry. Evangelism or social action without warfare prayer may have little impact in societies where the power of Satan has bound men and women in darkness for thousands of years. Paul explains in 2 Corinthians 4:4 that "the god of this age has blinded the minds of unbelievers, so that they cannot see the light of the gospel of the glory of Christ, who is the image of God." Before blinded unbelievers can respond to the truth of the Gospel, we must pray that the Holy Spirit will tear off the shroud of darkness the devil has placed over their minds.

Assisting with Development

Helping the needy in Window nations with food, economic development, medical assistance, and environmental assistance poses a direct threat to the evil powers that hold these people in captivity to poverty, famine, sickness, and disease. Recent events in the Republic of Benin show how believers can partner together to help develop a country both economically and spiritually.

Before the first *Praying Through The Window* initiative in 1993, the Republic of Benin was little known to many in the Christian world. As the body of believers started registering to pray for 10/40 Window countries, this small West African nation had been adopted by only 10 intercessors. No prayer journeyers were reported. At New Life Church in Colorado Springs, Colorado, a morning prayer group began to cry out for the Lord to move on the hearts of believers worldwide to pray for the Republic of Benin. When the initiative ended, the final tally showed that 103,000 intercessors had signed up to pray!

Two years later, as prayer journeyers from Ghana prepared to travel to Benin during *Praying Through The Window II*, God laid it upon their hearts to pray for Benin's former leader, Mathieu Kerekou. After the team arrived in Benin, local missionaries also asked them to pray for Kerekou, because he had recently become a Christian and an evangelist. The people of Benin wanted Kerekou to run again for president, but he was waiting for confirmation of God's will. The Ghanaian prayer journeyers joined the missionaries and Christians interceding for Kerekou's reelection. Soon afterwards, he announced his candidacy. God honored those prayers, and in March 1996 Kerekou was reelected president.

We were thrilled to hear that President Kerekou attended the July 1997 Global Consultation On World Evangelization (GCOWE) in Pretoria, South Africa. At the conference President Kerekou invited Christian businesspeople to join in creating an acceptable standard of living for all the people of Benin. Kerekou believes that Benin, while small, is strategically located and able to influence its West African neighbors to advance the kingdom of God. What kingdom vision from a head of state!

A month later, in August, 50 Christian businesspeople traveled to Benin at the invitation of President Kerekou to explore ways of assisting in the development of the country. Several socio/economic projects were formulated, which presently involve approximately 150 businesspeople from all around the world. Another group is exploring the opportunity of assisting Benin with major international investments. The goal is to invest one billion US dollars. Part of this investment strategy includes starting businesses among the unreached people groups in Benin and sharing the Gospel with them.

One of our challenges as the Church of Jesus Christ is to be on the cutting edge of establishing ministries that teach people how to care for the physical needs of their families and communities. Christian medical professionals must teach and promote basic hygiene in the Window countries so that people know how to avoid deadly bacteria through simple steps like washing hands after going to the toilet and not drinking water from the river where they bathe and rid themselves of bodily waste. Many 10/40 Window peoples lack adequate training in preventive medicine, first aid, and health care.

We need Christian agriculturists to teach people to grow their own food in sometimes difficult soil conditions and periodic drought. We need civil engineers to help design and build dams and to survey and prepare land for adequate living structures. We also need hydraulic engineers to help construct wells and environmental engineers to assist in making the water clean for drinking.

Engineering Ministries International (EMI), located in Colorado Springs, Colorado, embraces ministering the whole Gospel to the whole person, as expressed in their mission statement: "Mobilizing design professionals to minister to the less fortunate in developing nations, we proclaim the Gospel of Jesus by helping others change their world—through the development of hospitals, schools, orphanages, bridges, water supplies, electricity and more. Our commitment is to enrich the lives of those who give and those who receive."

Bi-vocational believers working with these kinds of ministries may live in places where they cannot openly share their faith, but they can show the love of Jesus through their lives. They can demonstrate that they are hard workers and people of high standards and moral character. In short, they can model the Rebecca principle—being willing to go the extra mile. In Genesis 24:15–20, we see how Rebecca did more than she was asked by giving Abraham's servant a drink *and* drawing water for his camels as well.

Because some believers in the 10/40 Window practice these virtues, CIN has received reports that governments hostile to the spread of the Gospel within their borders are openly looking for qualified Christian workers. Why? Believers have earned a reputation as being trustworthy, honest, and loyal, with an admirable work ethic.

Sending cutting-edge Christian professionals into spiritually resistant countries is a viable strategy to get the Gospel into Window countries. Their work will go a long way in breaking down demonic structures that have hindered the advance of the Gospel in these locations.

Assisting with Relief

The call for disaster relief often arises even more urgently than development needs. Disasters may stem from natural or human causes, but they usually demand swift response to prevent further destruction or loss of life. When Christians are prepared to go on site with help in the Name of Jesus, they have a wide-open opportunity to minister the love of God to desperate and suffering people.

The 10/40 Window countries suffer their share of natural disasters. Of the 26 major earthquakes this century, 11 have occurred in that region, along with five out of the 20 major volcanic eruptions.[5] Disasters in Window countries often have more devastating impact than elsewhere. The extreme poverty in Window countries means fewer local resources are available to assist suffering people and rebuild what was destroyed.

Proverbs 31:8-9 gives us a mandate for this ministry: "Speak up for those who cannot speak for themselves, for the rights of all who are destitute. Speak up and judge fairly; defend the rights of the poor and needy." We need more servant ministries doing relief work in the Name of Christ in the 10/40 Window. Some major agencies helping in this area include World Vision, World Relief Corporation, Operation Mobilization, Save The Children, Care, TEAR Fund (British), OXFAM (British), MSF (French-based "Doctors Without Borders"), Caritas (German Catholic service), CRS (Catholic Relief Service), World Council of Churches, Lutheran World Federation, Church World Service, and UMCOR.

Relief and development work has an impact in the spiritual as well as natural realm. Isaiah 58:6–12 explains how outreach to the oppressed, hungry, poor, and homeless actually releases the power and presence of God:

> Is not this the kind of fasting I have chosen:
> to loose the chains of injustice
>   and untie the cords of the yoke,
> to set the oppressed free and break every yoke?
> Is it not to share your food with the hungry
>   and to provide the poor wanderer with shelter—
> when you see the naked, to clothe him,
>   and not to turn away from your own flesh and blood?
> Then your light will break forth like the dawn,
>   and your healing will quickly appear;
> then your righteousness will go before you,
>   and the glory of the Lord will be your rear guard.
> Then you will call, and the Lord will answer;
>   you will cry for help, and he will say: Here am I.
>
> (vv. 6-9)

Our Response to the Call

How can each of us respond to the challenge of disarming the powers of darkness in the 10/40 Window? John Wesley is often quoted as saying, "God does nothing but in answer to prayer." The Holy Spirit looks for those who are praying and standing in the gap for the lost (Ezek. 22:30). Every believer is expected to pray. The Window nations will be transformed when we pray, take the Gospel message, meet physical needs, and make disciples, baptize them, and teach them how to obey God's command. If we don't fulfill our commission, Satan will rob these precious people from spending eternity with Christ.

The *JESUS* film team knows the difference that prayer makes in distribution of their videotapes. One film crew member testified, "Where effective prayer is brought before the Lord, more [of the film] is distributed." In a key port city, for instance, the team had great difficulty getting the film in. Although the port offered easy access with abundant evangelism opportunities, no one wanted to accept Christian materials there. The film distributors were moved to pray, and a breakthrough occurred. The team is convinced that receptivity mushrooms after on-site prayer.

Believers within the 10/40 Window also have responsibility to pray for their own nations, interceding for the power of God to disarm the demonic forces there. Indeed, national believers have more territorial authority than outsiders to conduct spiritual warfare in their land. The Body of Christ in each region must listen for the Lord's direction on when and how to take action, as when the Lord gave specific instructions to Gideon to pull down his father's altar to Baal, cut down the Asherah pole, and build an altar to the Lord (Judg. 6:25-27).

John Robb, in a phone interview on 5 June 1998, gave this example. In Calcutta, he says, the Church began interceding against corruption, historically a major problem in that city. Nationals took prayerwalks throughout Calcutta and at one point specifically prayed around a government building known for its corrupt officials. Some time later the building collapsed. The city then appointed a new and honest administrator to replace the previous corrupt one. Moreover, Calcutta in recent years has seen an increase in its overall cleanliness and a greater sense of compassion for the poor. Local intercessors attribute these changes to united prayer.

In Paul's enumeration of the armor of God in Ephesians 6:10-20, he tops off the list with prayer. In his article "Prayer Is

Social Action," John Robb notes Paul's emphasis: "In this struggle [against the powers of darkness], prayer is the decisive weapon, and it is often aggressive and violent. Karl Barth [the Swiss theologian] said, 'To clasp the hands in prayer is the beginning of an uprising against the disorder of the world.' The structures and forces of injustice, oppression, and war are so overwhelming, all our efforts to help the poor and needy will fall flat—unless we first invite God into the fray."[6] The Bible clearly describes prayer as the vehicle God uses to lay siege to demonic forces and to open the door to the Gospel message.

As we consider our role in ministering to a person's body, mind, and spirit, we must remember to keep all our efforts sustained in prayer if we hope to see eternal, spiritual transformation as part of the advance of God's kingdom. John Robb quotes theologian Walter Wink as saying, "The message is clear: History belongs to the intercessors, who believe the future into being.... God works with us and for us, to make and keep human life humane. And what God does depends on the intercessions of those who care enough to try to shape a future more humane than the present."[7]

God gave Ezekiel an awesome responsibility for the souls of those around him. "Son of man, I have appointed you a watchman to the house of Israel; whenever you hear a word from My mouth, warn them from Me. When I say to the wicked, 'You will surely die,' and you do not warn him or speak out to warn the wicked from his wicked way that he may live, that wicked man shall die in his iniquity, but his blood I will require at your hand. Yet if you have warned the wicked and he does not turn from his wickedness or from his wicked way, he shall die in his iniquity; but you have delivered yourself" (Ezek. 3:17–19, NAS).

Is the Spirit of the Lord still giving this charge to the Church today? Most definitely! His Word indicates that we have been appointed watchmen to pray, take the Gospel to the Window nations, and serve as a mouthpiece for the Holy Spirit.

God the Father empowered Jesus Christ to redeem fallen humanity and gave Him all authority in heaven and on earth.

Now Jesus has empowered and commissioned His Church to disarm the powers of darkness and take the Gospel message to every tribe, tongue, and nation. Will He say, "Well done, my good and faithful servants," to our generation?

You Can Help Meet the Challenge

- Commit to daily intercession and warfare prayer for the power of God to push back the strongholds of evil in 10/40 Window nations and pave the way for the advancement of the Gospel.

- Become informed about the desperate needs of people in the 10/40 Window who are trapped in poverty, sickness, and oppression. Pray for the Lord to intervene on their behalf.

- Support missionaries and Christian relief and development agencies that minister the Gospel to the whole person. Intercede for workers of these agencies regularly.

- Consider going on a short-term mission trip to the 10/40 Window to use your skills in areas such as medicine, engineering, agriculture, construction, education, business, and disaster relief.

Endnotes

1. Source: Verified and withheld; Church in Cleveland, Tennessee
2. John Robb with Larry Wilson, "In God's Kingdom…Prayer Is Social Action," *World Vision* magazine, February–March 1997, p. 4-7
3. Source: Verified and withheld; Report dated 7 June 1998
4. John Robb with Larry Wilson, "In God's Kingdom…Prayer Is Social Action," *World Vision* magazine, February–March 1997, p. 4
5. Source: *National Geographic*; Map of Natural Disasters
6. John Robb with Larry Wilson, "In God's Kingdom…Prayer Is Social Action," *World Vision* magazine, February–March 1997, p. 5
7. Ibid

5

Persecuted but Not Forsaken

*P*astor Paul James was a man of courage, full of energy and passion for his people. His church-planting efforts in the state of Orissa, India, bore remarkable fruit as he served as pastor for 15 churches. He also supervised the work of 15 other church planters who established nearly 100 churches. His vision was simple. He desired to see a church planted in every village in Orissa.

However, other forces were at work. Fanatical religious leaders opposed to the spread of Christianity determined to prevent Pastor James from any further success. He was beaten and told that if he didn't stop preaching the Gospel and converting the people, he would be murdered.

Concerned, Pastor James traveled with his wife and children to the home of K. A. Paul, his mentor and the one who had sent him out as a church planter. "What should I do," he asked his friend, "in light of the current threats and persecution?"

The two talked over the situation for the next few days. K. A. Paul related how he had been severely beaten and left for dead while ministering in the same state of Orissa. Pastor James was introduced to the gang leader, Maji, who was responsible for K. A. Paul's beating. Maji had been radically converted! Surrendering his life to Christ, he obeyed God's call to be a pastor in the village where he had instigated so much persecution.

After several days of prayer and counsel, Pastor James experienced renewed hope and courage. He knew God had called him to be a witness in this difficult region of Orissa. He couldn't forsake that call, even though the threats were very real and menacing. He knew he must go back, declaring boldly, "If I live, I live for Christ. If they kill me, let them kill me, but I will not turn back from Christ!"

Pastor James returned home with his family to face the challenges before him. A report came some months later about what had happened to the pastor. On 20 February 1994, his wife had an uneasy feeling that he should not go out that morning. But Pastor James felt he must go. As Pastor James was traveling, a crowd of religious fanatics brutally attacked him. The mob chopped at his limbs with an ax as he held up the Bible. When the fatal assault was over, his body had been cut into six pieces.

When his family was informed of the murder, one of Pastor James' daughters fell on K. A. Paul and cried, "Where is my father? Will you be my father now?"

In the midst of this tragedy, a special grace was evident. Mrs. James came from the Brahman caste, the highest social caste in India. She could easily have gone back to a life of relative ease if only she would forsake Christ. Yet her only request was that people pray for her children to follow Jesus into full-time ministry as their father had done. Today those prayers are being answered; her precious children are strongly committed to Christ.

Pastor Paul James could have done many things with his life. This talented man had a beautiful wife and three children who loved him dearly. Like his wife, he was from a high caste. He was the brother of a senator. He could have used his gifts to become a leading politician himself, or a successful businessman. But these things did not own him. Pastor James had surrendered his personal plans and direction to his Lord and Savior, Jesus Christ. His full allegiance was to the One who had freely given His life for us all. Pastor James was compelled to take the life-changing message of the Gospel to those who had never heard it. The lost must be reached, no matter the cost! No price was too great to be paid.[1]

Suffering for Christ

Persecution of Christians is on the rise all over the world. In some regions, pastors and their families are hunted like wild game. When captured, they undergo the kind of torture meted out in a prisoner-of-war camp. They are beaten and starved to death. Women are often raped and tortured while the men are forced to watch.

Following Christ in a country opposed to the Gospel brings immense hardships. Converts to Christianity are frequently forsaken by their families, who consider them dead and may even hold a funeral service for them. Even more appalling, some believers' kin put out death contracts for their lives. Some families kill the converts by crucifixion, beheading, drowning, stabbing, or live burial. What is their crime? They have chosen to follow the one true God.

The December 1997 *Advance* newsletter reported that A. T. Thomas, an Indian Catholic priest who worked among the lowest-caste Harijans, was kidnapped and beheaded in a forest in northern India's Bihar State. India Missions Association, meanwhile, told of the martyrdom of 22-year-old John Rajiv, an American who worked in India witnessing to his people. On 15 March 1998, Rajiv was stabbed to death by anti-Christians in Muzzafarpur in northern Bihar.

Non-Indians have no immunity. Youth With A Mission reported in their November 1996 *News Digest* that eight YWAM missionaries were attacked at their ministry training center in India after ignoring a death threat ultimatum. Five workers required hospitalization when a machete-wielding mob vandalized the center and tried to set the buildings on fire.

Yet the kingdom of God can prevail even in such situations. The eight YWAM workers refused to fight back when they came under attack. One of the injured told his attackers he forgave them. The men responsible for his wounds "broke down in tears," according to Jim Stier, current YWAM president. He attributed the peaceful result to "God's intervention and the enormous amount of prayer" raised by YWAM workers around the world who interceded during the crisis.

Persecution brings both sorrow and blessing. While the Church suffers, it also grows strong as it turns to Almighty God for spiritual resources. Unbelievers often stand convicted to see how Christians demonstrate faith and forgiveness in the midst of torture and even death. As the 3rd-century theologian Tertullian wrote in *Apologeticus,* "The blood of the martyrs is the seed of the Church."

Persecution and Church Growth in Iran

Events in Iran illustrate the doubled-edged nature of persecution. Prior to the Islamic Revolution, Christian missions had established 37 evangelical churches in Iran. In 1979, however, all Western missionaries were expelled. Despite—or because of—increasing persecution, phenomenal church growth has taken place. In 1977 there were 3,000 publicly registered Iranian Christians. By 1996 that number had grown to 20,000, at least half of them converts from Islam. Today, an estimated 120,000 unregistered believers live in Iran.

The *I.S.I.C. Bulletin* of December 1996–January 1997, from the Institute for the Study of Islam and Christianity, notes that "after the end of the war with Iraq in 1988, the Iranian regime concentrated on quelling religious dissent within Islam. The mullahs taught that Islam meant prosperity and peace for the country. During the war, however, many people began to question those claims. Protestant churches, on the other hand, preached the Good News of love and forgiveness. As a result, the number of converts to Christianity from Islam increased from 700 in 1980 to almost 6,000 by the cease-fire in 1988. This represents a growth of 857 percent"—growth that comes in the face of some of the world's most brutal religious repression.

The Iranian government has banned Protestant churches from holding services in Farsi, the national language. By doing this they have forced the churches, containing many converts from Islam, to cease activities or go underground. Many Christians are leaving the country because of fear and pressure. As one senior official at the Ministry of Islamic Guidance told a Christian, "From now on, either we kill all of you quietly or we make your lives so difficult that you will have no choice but to leave the country."

Open Doors tells the following story of martyrdom in its July 1997 newsletter:

In Sari, Iran, a gifted young evangelist and preacher named Mohammed Yusefi left his house for prayer at 6:00 a.m. on Saturday, 28 September 1996. He never returned. His body was found hanging on a tree in the forest near his home. There was clear evidence that he had also been tortured.

Yusefi was associated with the Assemblies of God churches in Iran's Mazandaran province, where he pastored three congregations. His fervency for evangelism and the discipling of new believers was responsible for the growth of the church in the nearby city of Gorgan.

Yusefi had been raising two sons of the late Rev. Mehdi Dibaj, who had been imprisoned for more than nine years for refusing to deny his faith in Christ. People opposed to Rev. Dibaj's incarceration and scheduled execution in January 1994 mounted a successful international campaign to have him freed. Five months after his release, however, 60-year-old Rev. Dibaj was murdered.

After Yusefi's body was released by the authorities, he was given a Christian funeral. This dedicated pastor was the seventh Christian leader to be martyred in Iran since the 1979 revolution. He was just 34 years old.

Such persecutions are not isolated incidents, yet they largely escape worldwide media scrutiny. Atrocities denounced by civilized people worldwide continue to be perpetrated today on innocent victims. According to an 8 October 1996 persecution report by Global Evangelization Movement (GEM), believers around the world are suffering untold hardships, humiliation, and murder. Christian churches have been riddled with gunfire, vandalized, torched, and burned to the ground. Recently nine believers in a 10/40 Window country were murdered when soldiers attacked them during worship. Hostile soldiers have butchered and mutilated Christian women, at times hacking off their breasts. Children are not exempt from the cruelty and horror of such suffering. There are reports from regions around the world that girls as young as six years have been raped by soldiers. Nine-year-old girls have been kidnapped and forced to marry old men. Women and young girls experience the outrage of gang rape by men representing anti-Christian governments. Other reports tell of Christian boys who are molested and castrated. Believers and their families are sold into slavery. Parents in some countries are forced to renounce their faith in Jesus Christ to keep their children from starving to death.

The Church's Suffering Foretold

From the time of the 1st-century Church, believers have experienced suffering and persecution at the hands of the enemies of the Gospel. A number of Scripture passages promise this as the lot of the Body of Christ. 2 Timothy 3:12 says, "Everyone who wants to live a godly life in Christ Jesus will be persecuted." In John 15:20, Jesus Himself declared, "If they persecuted me, they will persecute you also." Philippians 1:29 even indicates that suffering is a privilege: "For it has been granted to you on behalf of Christ not only to believe on him, but also to suffer for him."

Despite the cruelty, pain, and loss they experience, believers in the 10/40 Window know what it means to receive a blessing from persecution. Our Lord Jesus said in Matthew 5:10-11, "Blessed are those who are persecuted because of righteousness, for theirs is the kingdom of heaven. Blessed are you when people insult you, persecute you, and falsely say all kinds of evil against you because of me. Rejoice and be glad, because great is your reward in heaven, for in the same way they persecuted the prophets who were before you."

Persecuted believers have been tested and refined. Their experience reflects what the Apostle Paul described in 2 Corinthians 4:7-9 (NKJV): "But we have this treasure in earthen vessels, that the excellence of the power may be of God and not of us. We are hard pressed on every side, yet not crushed; we are perplexed, but not in despair; persecuted, but not forsaken; struck down, but not destroyed."

Persecution of the Church in Sudan

Sudan tops many lists of countries where violent persecution of Christians runs unchecked. The following article, "Sudan: Persecuted But Not Forsaken," appeared in the Fall 1997 *10/40 Window Reporter*.[2] The article describes the horrific circumstances in that country:

"Many kingdoms have risen and fallen in Sudan over the centuries, leaving several diverse identities—ethnic, cultural, and religious. When Sudan gained its independence in 1956, the structure of the new government ignored these diversities. Intolerance of religious differences became pronounced when soldiers led by Lt. Gen. Omar Ahmed al-Bashir seized power in Sudan in June 1989.

"Sweeping away a democratically elected government, the new regime promised a revolution of Islamic salvation. What they have delivered is a human rights disaster and an Islamic state of fear. Perhaps never in the history of Africa's largest country have Christians faced such a desperate situation. Millions of Christian families have fallen victim to the brutal treatment inflicted by an Islamic army set on *jihad*, Islamic holy war.

"Sudan is experiencing persecution unparalleled since the 1st-century Church. The Muslim regime's attempts to Islamize the entire population, poverty, and Christian infighting have taken the lives of nearly 3 million Sudanese. This government sanctions mass crucifixions, hangings, the burning of Christian villages and churches, and the sale of men, women, and children into slavery. This systematic persecution of the Sudanese people has forced millions to flee their homes. It was reported in *WindoWatchman,* published by Christian Information Network, that a Sudanese pastor asked, 'Why doesn't the Christian Church in the rest of the world raise its voice? We are strong in Christ, although we are hungry and thirsty and dying of disease.'

"As Christians, can we turn our backs on this horrific situation? Interfaith Christian Human Rights Alliance reports in their 25 July 1997 news release: 'There exists no greater example of base disregard for humanity than in Sudan today. Sudan has become the incubator of radical Islamic movements hosting at least 35 terrorist training bases, many staffed by Iranian revolutionary guards. And yet, no moral outrage has resulted in substantive actions to reverse the killing and enslaving. There is only silence and inaction.'

"Sudanese Christians who remain in occupied areas or in the Nuba Mountains face many cruelties. There have been reports of mass drownings in the Nile River. At one point, the river washed up an abominable 500 bodies in a single day! Christians have been set ablaze and then thrown into their church buildings. Soldiers often storm into homes and rape women in front of their entire families. Church leaders are sought out and captured, then lowered into dry wells and burned alive."

The *10/40 Window Reporter* article also details reports of persecution of Christian children. Boys are taken by force and sold as slaves or held in Islamic schools where they receive strict indoctrination in the teachings of Islam. Young girls have been taken from their families and sold as concubines or given to soldiers who use them to gratify their sexual desires. Untold thousands of children have simply disappeared. Many are believed to be hidden away by radical Muslims hoping to create a society emptied of any evidence of Christianity.

Currently, few steps are being taken to halt the horrific suffering of Sudanese Christians. Despite intense persecution, however, the Sudanese Church is reported to be the fastest growing church in the Muslim world. In light of this encouraging growth, ongoing Bible training and discipleship is desperately needed. Sudanese believers thirst to know more of God and His ways. *The 10/40 Window Reporter* article reports that after receiving just two weeks of training in the foundational truths of Christianity, one man was given 10,000 believers to pastor. Elsewhere, more than 300 Christians journeyed for 14 hours on foot to attend a pastors' conference held outside under mango trees. These believers endured the difficult journey to receive basic teachings on the character of God and Christian salvation.

The article continues:

"In 1996, missionaries went to a region in Sudan near the Nuba Mountains where it is estimated there is only one Bible for every three villages because of the extreme danger in getting into this area. In a special mission effort 1,500 Bibles were delivered by airplane. Planes have been shot down by militant Muslims to ensure this area remains isolated from the Gospel. Any mission work discovered means certain death for the workers. The regime uses systematic genocide, torture, and mass crucifixions to terrify all Sudanese citizens into conversion to Islam. Praise our God that despite the severe attacks, Sudanese Christians are continuing to press on toward the mark of the high calling of God."

Forgiveness: Changing the Destiny of a Persecuted Nation

We have personally heard Sudanese believers testify that God is using persecution in their land for His glory. In a conference that I (Beverly) attended, a Sudanese brother noted that persecution in the Bible always caused the believers to scatter, with the result that they shared their faith wherever they went. This is also true of the Sudanese Christians, who are sharing their faith as they are driven from their homes. Persecution has not hindered the Gospel but has served to enhance its spread!

This Sudanese brother said something I will never forget. He wanted us to pray not that persecution would stop but that believers would continue to be empowered by God to share the

Gospel everywhere they were scattered! I remember feeling amazed and challenged as I listened to his words. I questioned myself: Would the Lord find me this faithful if I were persecuted in this way? I prayed that he would.

My husband, Leonard, and I learned one of life's most important lessons during a trip overseas in 1997. The lesson began on a Sunday afternoon when I casually said to a Sudanese student I met, "My husband and I are staying here at the seminary. Perhaps we can get together with you and the other students while we're here to pray." He agreed and we met together the next morning.

What the students shared with us broke our hearts. We knew about Sudan's refugee camps—called "human zoos"— where Christian families were forced to renounce their faith in Jesus Christ in order to feed themselves and their children. We were told that the children in the camps were starving to death and only a thin layer of skin covered their little skeletons. We wept when one of the students told us how his mother was tied up and placed in the middle of the floor while Muslims repeatedly stabbed his brother until he died in front of her eyes. His brother's crime: converting from Islam to Christianity!

We had wondered why missionaries and relief agencies could not find a way to penetrate the Muslim soldiers' ironclad security barriers to smuggle food to these precious starving people.

We spent the day with the students. After a traditional Sudanese dinner, we enjoyed a time of prayer. They shared with us that there are more than one million Spirit-filled believers in Sudan. After I went to bed that night, their statement invaded my sleep, causing me to pray off and on until the next morning. I asked the Lord to reveal why so many Spirit-filled believers could not overcome the powers of darkness in their nation.

The next day we believe the Lord showed us one of the keys to destroying demonic strongholds in persecuted nations and in the lives of people held in bondage.

During our next meeting with the students, we discussed the importance of forgiving, praying for, loving, and blessing our enemies; loving those who are persecuting us; and praying for those in authority over us. I commented, "If we do not pray the will of God, we aren't praying any differently than the witch doctors."

I heard a gasp. Then a quiet voice responded, "We haven't been praying the will of God."

The Lord prompted me to say, "You need to forgive, pray for, and love those who are committing these horrific atrocities against the people in your country." I asked them, "Do you pray for those who are in authority over you and for those who are persecuting the Christians in Sudan?"

They answered, "We pray for them, but not in the way you're talking about." The students admitted later that they had been praying "like the witch doctors" and not in the way the Lord commands us to pray as believers for our enemies and oppressors.

The Lord had answered my prayer and shown me one of the reasons the Church of Jesus Christ in Sudan was in bondage. They had been cursing their enemies instead of obeying the instructions from the Word of God to bless them; they had been hating their enemies instead of loving them; they had been praying for ungodly things to happen to those in authority over them instead of praying for their salvation (Matt. 5:44, Rom. 12:14).

When the students understood the hardness unforgiveness had created in them, they repented (Matt. 6:14, 15). They went to the Word of God and prayed that the Lord would bring blessings and salvation to the Islamic regime. Then the students asked the Lord to soften their hearts to be able to love their enemies. As we prayed I saw a mental picture of a lock with a skeleton key. The key then entered the lock, and the Lord told me, "Forgiveness is one of the keys to changing the destiny of a persecuted nation."

The lesson we learned from these precious students is that no matter how terrible the things are that happen to us, we cannot allow them to fester in us. We must combat the sins of unforgiveness and hatred with Christ-empowered forgiveness. We must choose God's way, which is to forgive our enemies, and pray according to the Word of God.

Suffering and Evangelism in Indonesia

Indonesia is home to more Muslims than any other country in the world. Persecution of Christians in Indonesia has taken on new dimensions. According to the April/May 1997 *I.S.I.C. Bulletin,* church buildings have been destroyed at an average rate of one per week since 1992, totaling more than 200 Christian churches burned down by Muslim rioters.

On 10 October 1996 the first deaths from a church burning occurred when a pastor and four others in Situbondo, East Java, were trapped and killed during an attack on their church. Another pastor died in a church burning on 1 February 1997. Then, after the Asian financial crisis hit in late 1997, frustrated mobs widely targeted Chinese Christians with brutal violence, including looting, burning, gang rape, and murder.

Yet some believers see a silver lining. An e-mail from Jim Yost, an American national working in Indonesia, dated 10 May 1998 reports, "Just as in the Book of Acts, persecution has rallied the Church. Those who were riding the fence got off. And the rest are going for broke—especially in evangelism. I see greater emphasis in evangelism in Indonesia during these last years of more intense opposition."

In a telephone interview, Bruce Sidebotham, a former university professor in the province of West Sumatra, related the following stories from Indonesia:

"Personally I know of an old Gereja Protestant Indonesia Barat (GPIB) church in the city of Pariaman in West Sumatra that is in such rundown condition it is not possible to use it. The congregation has repeatedly petitioned the government for permission to repair the church, and the government refuses to grant the permits. The parishioners are forbidden to meet in homes and have to travel about 30 miles to go to a church in the city of Padang.

"The GPIB church in Padang is too small to hold its congregation. Every Sunday, rain or shine, chairs are set up in the yard outside to handle the overflow. Repeatedly the congregation has tried to get permission to expand their church, and permission is never granted. It is not denied either, but the process to get permission never ends.

"Back in 1994 I personally watched a young Pentecostal evangelist die in the intensive care unit of the Catholic hospital in Padang. I did not take pictures through the window because there was a plain-clothes policeman outside his room and I was afraid my camera would be confiscated. The evangelist had been ministering on the mostly Christian Mentawai Islands that are administered from West Sumatra. He was accused of having burned a Qu'ran when he burned the charms of a witch doctor whom he converted. The police arrested him and took him to Pariaman. He was in good shape when he was arrested. A week later he turned up in the Catholic hospital in Padang in a coma. His face was black and blue, swollen to the size and shape of a cantaloupe. He had burn marks on his wrists, caused from either lighted cigarettes or electric wires. His whole body was black and blue."

Martyrdom in the 20th Century

In Matthew 24:6-7, Jesus Christ said that the last days would be marked by "wars and rumors of wars…nation [rising] against nation, and kingdom against kingdom. There will be famines and earthquakes in various places." Verse 9 plainly tells us that we will be persecuted and put to death and hated by all nations because of Him.

Persecution and martyrdom are common in the 10/40 Window. Christian Solidarity International, a global interdenominational organization that defends the human rights of persecuted believers and other victims of repression, has developed a map showing the countries with restricted human rights in colors on four levels. The darker the color, the fewer human rights are honored. Within the three levels of more restricted human rights are all the countries in the 10/40 Window. Most believers in countries where freedom of religion is observed are unaware of the hideous crimes launched against Christians in other nations.

The statistics from GEM/World Evangelization Research Center are staggering. In 1997 an estimated 160,000 believers were killed for their faith. This means that every day logs an average of 438 Christian martyrs, most of them in the 10/40

Window. Since 1900, more people have been killed for believing in Jesus than were killed in all the wars fought this century.

In the GEM publication *Monday Morning Reality Check*, managing editor Justin Long reports that "martyrdom across the ages has garnered a significant amount of interest recently. In *Our Globe and How to Reach It* (1990, Barrett & Johnson), the grim facts are presented. From AD33 to 1990, there were 420 situations of martyrdom (where large groups of Christians are killed). In 56 of these incidents, over 100,000 were killed; in 20, more than half a million were killed; and in 12 over 1 million were killed. The bulk of these situations occurred in two periods: the first, between AD1000 and 1500, and the second, a much shorter period, between 1900 and 1980. Approximately 26 million, more than half of all Christian martyrs ever, were killed in this latter period. Some 9.9 million were martyred in the past 40 years alone."[3]

In conversation with David B. Barrett on 15 December 1998, I (Luis) asked him how he calculated the number of martyrs. He explained that a list has been compiled of all situations of martyrdom. The list of reported martyrs has been documented going back to AD33. For example, in Sudan close to two million were listed over the past thirty years. One-half million were added during Amin's rule in Uganda in the seventies. Fifteen million were added to this list from the period of Stalin's rule in the former USSR from 1929 to 1953. When the average number of Christian martyrs per year is calculated, those who are added to the list meet the following criteria: a believer in Christ who loses his or her life prematurely in a situation of witness as a result of human hostility.

Revelation 12:10-11 tells us that those willing to die for their faith will see a great final victory over the devil: "Then I heard a loud voice in heaven say: 'Now have come the salvation and the power and the kingdom of our God, and the authority of his Christ. For the accuser of our brothers, who accuses them before our God day and night, has been hurled down. They overcame him by the blood of the Lamb and by the word of their testimony; they did not love their lives so much as to shrink from death.'"

Keeping the Faith in China

The suffering of believers in China since the Communist takeover in 1949 has been well documented. The August 1997 *Advance* newsletter gives a typical report: "About 40 house church leaders were arrested and 200 buildings demolished or closed in June 1997, when Chinese authorities cracked down on unregistered congregations in Wenzhou, China. Wenzhou has one of the highest concentrations of Christians in China, with at least 600,000 believers in a population of 7 million."

With Christians arrested and imprisoned regularly, it is mind-boggling that the Church in China has grown from an estimated one million believers in 1949 to somewhere between 60 and 120 million today.

A prayer journey team from Fairbanks, Alaska, went to China in July 1997 and had an opportunity to interview an elderly Chinese man who knows the meaning of suffering. Here is his story, as told in the prayer journey report:

"How did you find encouragement during your time in prison?"

"I prayed every day; even when I was working, my mind was doing God's work.... I continued to preach in prison, locked in a very small room over one year. For 130 days my wrists were handcuffed, tied very close together. The handcuffs dug into my flesh. I had blisters from being pushed and pulled by the handcuffs. It was a long way to the bathroom. Many people would beat me. I would ask them if they knew Jesus....They beat me more.

"I said, 'Lord, I have followed you.' The meaning of my life was for mission work in China. I thought, why should I live when I can't honor the Lord? I decided if I would commit suicide, I would see Jesus. So I prayed one day and one night, and decided to get on the bed and electrocute myself. I tried, but the power wasn't strong enough. The iron handcuffs wouldn't let the power be strong enough.

"Two people would bring me meals. The people saw what I had tried to do to punish the government. The government said that since I believed in God so much, there was no hope I would change. I was kicked and punched and beaten for 47 days, three times a day. God's grace saved me. I'm still saved. Then I said, 'I'm too weak, Lord; why did I try to commit suicide?' I prayed and I repented. The Lord said, 'My grace is enough for you.' The third time He said it I cried.

"I have had many more experiences, but we don't have enough time. The head of the prison camp once asked me, 'If someone hits you in the face, do you let them? Is this correct? Do you allow them to walk all over you?' I could only agree. 'When you meet a robber, because you are too weak, you turn the other cheek and let him take your tunic—one day when you get strong enough you should avenge.' No, I told him; I do not avenge because I am a Christian.

"I am 78 years old. I have no worries. I will die for the Lord. I would like to give up myself to the Lord. It is God's perfect plan that I am still alive in China. People offered to bring me to a big church in the States. They offered me a ministry in California. I have all the required paperwork to go, but the Lord has me stay here. This is His perfect plan. I am willing to stay to do what I can do."[4]

Crackdown on Christians in Saudi Arabia

Saudi Arabia, birthplace of Islam and guardian of its holiest cities, is extremely hostile to Christianity. Churches are forbidden. Neither Saudis nor expatriates may display Christian artifacts, symbols, or literature. Police seek out and raid secret worship services taking place in private homes. Hundreds of foreign and national workers have been imprisoned for their faith, with many tortured and many deported.

In June 1998, agents of the Saudi Ministry of Interior arrested three Filipino Christians for distributing Christian literature. The probe expanded, and more than a dozen others were brought in for interrogation. Some had their homes searched and computer databases confiscated. A Dutch citizen working in Saudi Arabia was arrested on 13 June as part of the crackdown. The 35-year-old businessman was denied diplomatic access and held incommunicado from his family for many days.

Authorities also detained and interrogated Yolanda Aguilar, the wife of a Filipino fellowship leader, while her husband was outside the country. Nine months pregnant, she was held under a form of house arrest at the hospital compound where she soon gave birth.

Sources alerted Christians in other countries to pray and to write Saudi Arabian embassies worldwide to protest this treatment. One month later, God answered prayers. Over the course of a week in mid-July the government began releasing and deporting these Christian prisoners to their home countries. Yolanda Aguilar's confiscated passport was returned so she could apply for an exit visa for herself and her newborn daughter, later joining her husband in the Philippines.

"Freedom of religion does not exist," the U.S. State Department's 1997 Human Rights Report on Saudi Arabia declares. "Islam is the official religion, and all citizens must be Muslims. The government prohibits the public practice of other religions."

Church Expansion amid Opposition in Nepal

In a 1998 report, a reliable source supplied the following transcript of a taped interview with a woman we will call Mannu, who helped pioneer a Christian ministry in Nepal with her husband starting in 1973. Working with another missionary couple, they translated the Bible into Nepalese. In the early 1970s there were only about 200 known Christians in the country. Now there are more than 500,000. The church has grown tremendously, especially through the testing and persecution they have encountered. Here are stories from Mannu's May 1998 report, "What God Does in the Midst of Persecution":

"In l989, [my husband] Adon was arrested with other church leaders and put in prison for one month, then released on bail. We were watched at all times. Prayer was the only thing we could gather and be able to do with others. All the house churches in Kathmandu were closed. The Supreme Court was going to arrest Adon again and put him in jail for six years, so our Christian leadership encouraged him to leave the country. Adon left Nepal and went down to India. But I had a very specific instruction from the Lord that I had to stay in Nepal. I knew the king was the final authority and that even though the Supreme Court had made a decision, I could appeal to the king. So I appealed to him on behalf of my husband. Many of us were praying and crying unto the Lord on my husband's behalf to do a miracle. Adon was in India for one year. Yet within the year, in 1990, democracy took over and all religious prisoners were released.

"In 1990 we had only nine churches in Kathmandu. Now we have 145! We are growing very fast. Some years ago I was asked how we train our pastors, whether or not they had been to school, or if they could read or write. Some of the pastors are shepherding 30 or 40 congregations in the remote areas.

"One pastor came to our house many years ago. He brought a bag of small rocks. 'Since it is so difficult to count the numbers of those baptized,' he said, 'I keep a bag of rocks. This is how many I have baptized.' We counted the stones, and there were 75. Another time he came with 130 rocks in his bag.

"Persecution brings many people to the Lord. As an example, here is one story. We have a pastor who used to be an alcoholic. He used to come home drunk every day. He didn't have a job. His wife and daughter suffered also, but somehow they heard the Gospel and became Christians. Every evening they went to a secret prayer fellowship or Bible study. The husband found out that they were meeting every evening and became very suspicious about their activities. He imagined they were engaging in bad business, or something to get money from people. He vowed, 'I am not going to drink tonight and I will follow them to see where they are going.'

"When he saw his wife and daughter go out, he followed behind. He saw them go into a house and the door shut behind them. He crept close and tried to eavesdrop to know what was going on inside.

"Somehow, at the same time, the police had heard that these believers were gathering in this house. When they arrived, they arrested this man. They thought he was the leader and that he was protecting those gathered inside, allowing them to have the meeting. So they took him away.

"It was a long three- to four-hour walk to the police station. The police were smoking, and this man said to the officers, 'Can I have a cigarette?'

"The police looked at him and said, 'Don't give me that—Christians don't smoke. Don't pretend that you are not a Christian; we are not going to release you.'

"So they continued to walk. On the way he also saw the house where he would often stop and get his alcohol. He asked the police, 'Can we stop here so I can go to this house for a while and have a drink?'

"Again the police responded, 'Don't pretend—we know Christians don't drink. We are not going to stop here; we are going to send you to the prison.' So without any trial or anything, he was put into prison for two years.

"The man's wife and daughter did not know what had happened to him. It took two weeks before they heard word, since there is no means of communication. They learned that he had been arrested for being a Christian. This news thrilled the mother and daughter, who thought, 'Our prayers have been answered!' So they went to visit him and said, 'We are Christians, and you didn't let us know that you have become a Christian. We are so excited.'

"The man became angry. He told them, 'I don't know what Christian means, or how you become Christian. I don't know anything about that.'

"His wife answered, 'You read your Bible, and you invite Jesus into your life.'

"He asked her to bring him a Bible. And after two years he came out of prison a very fine Christian. He calls himself 'a government-made Christian.' He is a strong believer, very bold, and is pastoring a very strong church. And since he had served his term, they couldn't arrest him again!"

Widespread Suffering, Vibrant Growth

Other nations of the 10/40 Window generate similar stories of believers who suffer and yet persevere under trials and persecutions. On 12 January 1998, militant Islamic assailants killed Rev. Vasilios Haviaropoulos, the 73-year-old caretaker of an

Orthodox Church in downtown Istanbul, Turkey. On 14 December 1997, a mob of about 600 Buddhists attacked an Assemblies of God church in Matara, in the southern region of Sri Lanka, during a Sunday morning service. They smashed the church windows, assaulted the believers, and damaged and overturned vehicles outside. On 10 February 1997, two Assyrian Christians in Northern Iraq, a father and son, were killed by a mob of 200 Kurdish Muslims in the streets of Shaqlawa, near Arbil.

Compass Direct's 18 March 1997 news release, along with Barnabas Fund, Speed the Need, and others, told of an incident that took place in southern Egypt. On 12 February 1997, suspected Muslim extremists stormed into a Coptic Christian church in the village of El-Fikriya, near Abu Qurqas, and opened fire with automatic rifles. The gunmen killed ten people and wounded five, two of whom later died of their wounds. Most of the victims were young students attending a youth meeting in the Margy Guirguis church. Extremists routinely force Coptic Christian villagers in Upper Egypt to either pay them "protection money" or be killed.

During the first week of February 1997, at least 13 churches and several other Christian buildings were burned in the Christian-majority town of Shanti Nagar, near Khanewal, Pakistan. The Barnabas Fund's March 1997 newsletter, *Voice of the Martyrs,* and others reported this atrocity. About 75 percent of the town was destroyed in the attack by more than 30,000 angry Muslims, after imams announced unproved allegations that a Christian had desecrated a copy of the Qu'ran. (Later, it was confirmed that police were responsible for starting this rumor.) About 1,500 homes were razed, while possessions, agricultural tools, and livestock were stolen or burned, and pumps and water tanks wrecked. Around 30,000 Christians were left homeless. This was by far the most serious attack on Christians in Pakistan since the nation gained its independence 50 years ago. An urgent appeal went out to supply the basic needs of these newly-destitute Christians. Barnabas Fund noted that "the name Shanti Nagar means 'Community of Peace'—but there is no peace in Shanti Nagar."

According to an internal report of the World Evangelical Fellowship (WEF), leaders of the underground house churches in southern Vietnam face strict fines and other repressive measures, including long prison sentences. Yet these house churches are experiencing vibrant growth. "Their membership has doubled or even tripled in the last few years, and now stands at about 80,000."[5]

The Church in Bhutan tells an even more amazing story of growth in the midst of persecution. A 1997 report from the Jesuit Refugee Service describes the situation:

"It is illegal for the Bhutanese to embrace any religion but Buddhism, and it is illegal to evangelize. [Foreign] companies cannot do business in the country unless the government invites them to do so.

"An ethnic cleansing was carried out in the country in April 1993. Thousands of Indian, Nepalese, Tibetan, and Bangladeshi Bhutanese were driven out of the country. At this time, it was discovered that about 500 Christians lived in the country. All but 100 were expelled, removed, or imprisoned.

"Today, there are 10,000 Bhutanese Christians. This dramatic growth from only 100 remaining Christians in October 1993 shows the result of united, focused prayer and outreach. But the persecution is still severe and covers almost all of the social and economic life of the believers. Christians are fired from their jobs and cannot be hired by other Bhutanese. This makes economic survival very difficult for them, since only Bhutanese can own businesses in Bhutan."[6]

The Church's Response

As believers, what should be our response to these accounts of persecution? The most powerful response is prayer. God can work His will in even the most impossible situations.

Active support of mercy ministries, relief organizations, and refugee programs can also reach many people being persecuted for their faith and beliefs. We can also hold repressive governments accountable for their actions. Approximately 60 countries of the 10/40 Window belong to the United Nations and thus subscribe to its Universal Declaration of Human Rights. Article 18 of that document states: "Everyone has the right to freedom of thought, conscience and religion; this right includes freedom to change his religion or belief, and freedom, either alone or in community with others and in public or private, to manifest his religion or belief in teaching, practice, worship, and observance."

There are many ways God could burden our hearts with compassion for believers in other countries who are suffering injustices. Yet we must remember how the Holy Spirit works powerfully through suffering and pray according to His Word and His will alone. Jeff Beacham's *JB Report* cited this startling quotation from David White of Harvest Ministries International: "A ministry in the U.S. that supplies Bibles to China recently printed a message from one of the leaders in the underground church. Nearly 90 percent of all believers in China are part of the underground church. He requested that believers in America continue to send Bibles; however, he specifically asked the church in America not to pray that the persecution of the church in China would stop. He said that persecution actually helped them to stay close to God."[7]

What can we say to this? Perhaps the United States and other Western countries need a bigger dose of persecution! Many of us would find it difficult to conclude with Hezekiah in Isaiah 38:17, "Surely it was for my benefit that I suffered such anguish," or to respond as Peter and his friends did in Acts 5:41: "The apostles left the Sanhedrin, rejoicing because they had been counted worthy of suffering disgrace for the Name."

Christians in the 10/40 Window can identify with 1 Peter 1:6-7: "In this you greatly rejoice, though now for a little while you may have had to suffer grief in all kinds of trials. These have come so that your faith—of greater worth than gold, which perishes even though refined by fire—may be proved genuine and may result in praise, glory, and honor when Jesus Christ is revealed."

We praise God for bringing such good from evil. At the same time, our hearts cry out to God for mercy on His suffering children. Even so, come quickly, Lord Jesus!

You Can Help Meet the Challenge

- Become informed about persecutions and atrocities against Christians occurring around the world.
- Pray daily for suffering believers in the 10/40 Window nations.
- Ask God to turn the hearts of the persecutors and oppressors towards repentance and salvation in Jesus Christ.
- Mobilize your church to support the annual International Day of Prayer for the Persecuted Church each November.
- Hold governments accountable for human rights abuses in their countries, especially in the name of religion, by contacting their embassies and letting them know you are actively watching their decisions. Remind those who are members of the United Nations that Article 18 of the U.N. Declaration on Human Rights promotes freedom of religion.
- Pray that God will show business people innovative ways to start businesses and hire Christians in persecuted countries.
- It has been said that in some poor countries a family only needs US $27 to start a business and feed their families. Pray that ministries and entrepreneurial missionaries will be used of God to help the poor by finding them jobs and by starting small businesses.

Endnotes

1. Source: Gospel to the Unreached Millions, Houston, Texas; from e-mail of 10 August 1998
2. Source: "Sudan: Persecuted But Not Forsaken," *10/40 Window Reporter,* Fall 1997. This article cites "Mission Sudan" in *The Voice of the Martyrs,* July 1997; Friday Fax; and the Interfaith Christian Human Rights Alliance.
3. Justin Long, "Christian Martyrdom," *Monday Morning Reality Check #2,* January 1996
4. Source: Name verified and withheld
5. DAWN Friday Fax #10.97, 14 March 1997
6. www.jesuit.org
7. Jeff Beacham, *JB Report,* 7 September 1998, firepowerministries@msn.com

6

The Nicodemuses
Come at Night

*L*ate one evening in 1st-century Judea, a man of wealth and prominence arranged a private meeting with Jesus. Nicodemus, a well-respected Pharisee and a member of the Jewish ruling council, came seeking truth, eager to know more about this new spiritual leader. John 3:1-21 records their conversation. Although he did not understand all of what Jesus had to say, Nicodemus' first comment reflected his receptivity: "Rabbi, we know you are a teacher who has come from God. For no one could perform the miraculous signs you are doing if God were not with him" (v. 2).

As a ruling Pharisee among Jewish leaders hostile to Jesus' ministry, Nicodemus probably took a great risk in seeking out the Lord. His coming at night may reflect his desire to remain a behind-the-scenes follower. In John 7:50-51 Nicodemus, without acknowledging his viewpoint, spoke a cautionary word before the council in defense of Jesus ("Does our law condemn anyone without first hearing him to find out what he is doing?"), and was rebuked by his peers. Nonetheless, almost three years after his nighttime visit, Nicodemus boldly and publicly came forward after the crucifixion to claim the body of Jesus. He was accompanied by Joseph of Arimathea, another leader who had been a secret disciple of Jesus (John 19:38). Nicodemus brought about 75 pounds of costly spices, and the two wrapped Jesus' body with the spices in strips of linen before placing it in the tomb (John 19:39-42).

In the 10/40 Window today, many "Nicodemuses" quietly pursue truth. The modern-day Nicodemuses are men, women, and even children of great influence, position or wealth. Some would call them "mind molders"—people who are destined to shape society. In some cases they may not yet know the one true God, but they are already seeking Him with open hearts. God wants them in His service to impact many others for His purposes. Through strategically-placed Nicodemuses and their leadership influence, the Holy Spirit can transform whole segments of society to know and revere Jesus.

Many Nicodemuses are religious leaders from non-Christian backgrounds. Some are nominal Christians who hold positions of influence; among them are kings and their families, heads of state, politicians, scientists, doctors, lawyers, engineers, businesspeople, the rich and famous, media barons, intellectuals, and college professors. Some are born-again believers who have chosen not to use their influence to advance the kingdom of God. Others are believers who are currently being used powerfully by God. All know, as did Nicodemus of old, what it means to have an encounter with the Sovereign Lord.

God-Inspired Dreams

An amazing story about a prominent governmental official of a Middle Eastern country was recounted by the DAWN Friday Fax:

This official, whose debaucherous lifestyle had created international headlines for years, was bedridden for some time in 1997 after being shot. A young Christian we will call Rahkma "saw herself explaining the Gospel to him in a dream." The dream made such an impression that the woman, a poor refugee, immediately set off on her way to the official's office.

"I have a message for…[name withheld] from Jesus Christ, which I can only give him verbally," she told the office security guards.

The guards initially suspected an unusual joke, but Rahkma persisted until one of them began to relent.

"Jesus Christ is a well-known person," one of the guards said, "so perhaps we should let the woman in." The guard telephoned the official. "There's a woman here who claims to have a message for you from Jesus Christ. We can't get rid of her. What should we do?"

The official told his secretary to send Rahkma to him in his limousine. She spent two hours with him and not only explained the Gospel to him but also prayed with him to invite Jesus into his life. According to the report, the man was crying as he prayed.

"What can I do for you or your family?" he asked.

"Nothing," replied Rahkma, giving him a Bible. "I'm simply your sister now."

It would be easy to assume that this prominent official would never speak publicly about his experience with Jesus because of his country's religious and political climate. However, during a televised speech some days after his meeting with Rahkma, he spoke out for increased tolerance towards Christians.

This same young woman was involved in a second amazing story reported in the same Friday Fax. Rahkma traveled to Sudan following another dream in which "Jesus asked her to go to Khartoum" to explain the Gospel to the Muslim head of state, General Omar al-Bashir. Christian aid agencies tell of up to 1.5 million martyrs who have died since the start of the civil war in Sudan. Bashir has been known for his fiery sermons from the Qu'ran.

Rahkma received her opening through General al-Bashir's sister, an acquaintance. Rahkma told her that the Lord had sent her to speak to the general. But the woman replied that she had not seen her brother for quite some time. After a long wait, the general's sister arranged for Rahkma to attend a family celebration, even though she did not expect her brother to come.

By God's grace, General al-Bashir did attend the gathering. He was just heading out of the house after an urgent telephone call when Rahkma got her chance. "You have one minute," he said.

"I have a message for you from Jesus Christ," Rahkma told him. "If everything were taken from you, General—power, money, health—what would you do, and who would help you? Jesus Christ is always there for you!"

One minute turned into 40, and al-Bashir listened astonishedly to the Gospel. At the end of the time, he asked Rahkma to pray for him.

We don't know whether the general asked Jesus into his heart, but observers consider this event unprecedented. Sudanese Christians informed us that, shortly afterwards, restrictions on Christian meetings in Northern Sudan were "inexplicably lifted by someone in high position."[1]

"I Summon You…Though You Do Not Acknowledge Me"

Stories like these are emerging from many countries. Both Christian leaders and Christians with "no name recognition," like Rahkma, are gaining audiences with high-level leaders and kings of the earth, preaching the Gospel and prophesying to them. In some cases these people of influence have had vivid or troubling dreams they cannot understand. Like Pharaoh of ancient Egypt, they inquire until they find a modern-day "Joseph" to come interpret for them (Gen. 41).

In the 21st century, we will witness a multitude of Nicodemuses who will be used of God. Some will know Jesus. Some will not. The non-believers whom the Holy Spirit enlists will function much like King Cyrus in the Old Testament. Although Cyrus did not acknowledge the one true God, the Lord used him to carry out His will. According to Isaiah 44:28–45:7,

[I am the Lord] who says of Cyrus, "He is my shepherd
    and will accomplish all that I please;
he will say of Jerusalem, 'Let it be rebuilt,'
    and of the temple, 'Let its foundations be laid.'"
This is what the Lord says to his anointed,
    to Cyrus, whose right hand I take hold of…:
For the sake of Jacob my servant,
    of Israel my chosen,
I summon you by name
    and bestow on you a title of honor,
    though you do not acknowledge me.
I am the Lord, and there is no other;
    apart from me there is no God.
I will strengthen you,
    though you have not acknowledged me,
so that from the rising of the sun
    to the place of its setting
men may know there is none besides me.
    I am the Lord, and there is no other.

Ezra 1:1-8 says that "the Lord moved the heart of Cyrus king of Persia to make a proclamation" that the Temple should be rebuilt and that the Jews in exile should have liberty to return to Jerusalem for the work. Then in Ezra 6:1-12, a subsequent Persian king, Darius the Great, followed Cyrus' lead by issuing a similar decree. Darius provided all the resources needed to finish the rebuilding and offer the required sacrifices.

God chose these Nicodemuses before the foundations of the earth. Psalm 139:15 teaches that God "formed them in the secret place." He planted in them aptitude and gifting as well as the option to take the path of His divine will for their lives. King Cyrus, for instance, had a choice to be used by God or to go his own way. He chose to let God use him.

Disenchantment hovers over the lives of Nicodemuses who are not fulfilling God's purposes for them. The Holy Spirit is wooing them to follow the path that will place them in areas where they will accomplish God's will. Many of these Nicodemuses have come to the end of themselves and reliance on their own intellect, resources, and ideas. While they may enjoy great achievement, an aching void haunts their existence. Some have tried every strategy of the secular world. They have gone by the books. They have used the formulas guaranteed to bring success. In many cases the formulas have produced for them what they thought they were looking for, but things are still not right. These Nicodemuses feel empty inside, devoid of purpose and direction.

When these chosen ones come to know the Lord, as well as acknowledge the hand of the Lord and His calling on their lives, they will find fulfillment at last. But that is not all. The Nicodemuses who decide to follow the leading of the Holy Spirit will be used powerfully to spread the Gospel to the ends of the earth.

A Transforming Vision of Jesus

From contacts in North Africa comes this account told in Jane Rumph's book, *Stories from the Front Lines: Power Evangelism in Today's World:*

In a city in Egypt, a Christian woman we will call Eman received an invitation around November 1994 that made her tremble with fear.

Is this a trap? she wondered.

She had been asked to pray for a sick woman at the home of a devout and influential Muslim leader. The ill woman knew Eman to be a Christian, and Eman knew that most Muslims recognize Isa (Jesus) as a healer. But Eman had no idea what she was getting into.

Feeling a little like Ananias being sent by God to pray for Saul, the enemy of the early Church, Eman drove to the home of the Muslim leader, whom we will call Mohammed Ibrahim. After a short time at the house praying for the woman, Eman hurried back to her car, eager to make her escape. To her horror, Ibrahim followed her out. He forced himself into her car and shut the door.

"I have something very important to tell you," he said in a low voice.

Eman's heart pounded as she listened, every nerve on guard. Ibrahim confessed in strictest confidence that he led an underground fundamentalist Islamic group pledged to destroy all the Christian churches in that city.

"But the week before last, I was visited in the night by a very moving vision," he revealed. "Isa appeared to me in my bedroom as a bright white figure. He showed me the wound holes in His hands and feet. He spoke and said, 'I have shed My blood also for you. I want you to build My Church, not to destroy it.'"

Ibrahim paused. "I was so transformed by this vision that I decided to become a follower of Isa al Masih [Jesus the Messiah]."

Eman's shock only grew deeper.

Ibrahim went on to explain that he had recounted his vision to his group, and to his astonishment all 150 people agreed to follow his decision. The members, already underground, now committed themselves covertly to advance the work of the Church. Eman, filled with wonder, hardly had words to express her praise for God's glory.[2]

Stories like this indicate that God Himself is orchestrating events towards the goal of fulfilling the Great Commission. God has mandated our involvement in the work, but His sovereign power determines the outcome. In the words of Jonathan in 1 Samuel 14:6, "Nothing can hinder the Lord from saving, whether by many or by few."

Even though some Nicodemuses, like the Egyptian leader in this story, operate under cover now, when the fire gets hot many will be bold and courageous to stand up and be counted with the saints of the Most High God. In the crucible of public hostility on the day of Jesus' crucifixion, it was Nicodemus—not the disciples—who went with Joseph to recover the body of our Lord. These two men of influence put their lives, fame, and reputations on the line. Today's Nicodemuses also are often men and women of courage. They are accustomed to operating on the front lines, and in the end they will stand up for their beliefs.

"Nicodemuses" in the Bible

The Bible gives many examples of leaders who vocally defended faith in the one true God.

Because of his intelligence, wisdom, and strength of character, the young man Daniel was promoted to high position in the kingdom of Babylon during the Jewish exile. Never once did he deny his faith; in fact, he practiced it openly and suffered persecution as a result. Jealous administrators "tried to find grounds for charges against Daniel in his conduct of government affairs, but they were unable to do so. They could find no corruption in him, because he was trustworthy and neither corrupt nor negligent" (Dan. 6:4). Daniel's integrity and open devotion to God, even in the face of unjust laws targeting him for his faith, influenced the king so deeply that the spiritual atmosphere of the entire kingdom changed:

> Then King Darius wrote to all the peoples, nations and men of every language throughout the land:
> "May you prosper greatly!
> "I issue a decree that in every part of my kingdom people must fear and reverence the God of Daniel.
> "For he is the living God
>   and he endures forever;
>   his kingdom will not be destroyed,
>   his dominion will never end"
>   (Dan. 6:25–26).

Queen Esther also stood up for her faith at a crucial time when she could have lost her life for revealing her loyalties. Although God had raised her to the highest position for a woman in the Persian kingdom, no one but her cousin Mordecai knew she was a Jew who believed in the one true God. When wicked Haman schemed to destroy all the Jews in the kingdom, Esther knew she had to summon her courage and go to the king with the truth. At the risk of death she pleaded in defense of her people and her faith (Esther 7:3-4), and God brought complete vindication.

In the New Testament, the wife of Pontius Pilate, governor of Judea, made an impassioned plea to her husband on behalf of Jesus, who was then on trial before the governor. As far as we know she was not a believer, but she had received a divinely-sent dream warning Pilate not to have anything to do with his innocent defendant (Matt. 27:19). Her role as the governor's wife gave her access to him, and she was willing to speak up on behalf of truth and righteousness.

In Acts 8, the Holy Spirit gave Philip a divine appointment with an Ethiopian eunuch, an important official in the court of the Ethiopian queen. The Spirit had already softened the heart of this devout man, who sought God fervently and searched the Scriptures for truth. Philip opened the Word to his understanding and led him to faith in Messiah Jesus. Upon being baptized, the official returned to his country rejoicing. In his position of influence, he likely shared the Good News with a network of many others of high status.

"Nicodemuses" in Our Day

Chapter 4 recounted that Mathieu Kerekou, the president of the West African nation of Benin, came to faith in Christ a few years ago. A pastor from Benin's Evangelical Association was instrumental in leading Kerekou to salvation. Kerekou has become an outspoken advocate of the Gospel. When the former Marxist dictator was reelected president in March 1996 after a period out of office, he dedicated his country to Christ at his inauguration.

The 10/40 Window Reporter relates how God is using one of today's Nicodemuses as a modern-day Cyrus: "In a bold stand for religious freedom, King Hussein of Jordan has ordered government schools to offer Bible study to Christian students, instead of forcing them to study the Qu'ran. This is a major step for Jordan, which is a predominantly Muslim country. Christians account for only 5 percent of its 3.8 million people.

"Pray that God will prosper King Hussein for his courageous stand. Pray also that God would grant believers the boldness in His Spirit to witness as He leads them—and that He would provide them with divine appointments to share their faith. According to sources, proselytizing is no longer against the law."[3]

Local leaders are also being used by God. The story of a Nigerian clan chief who made a bold appeal after God spoke to him in a dream is recounted by Mark Kelly in the November 1997 *Advance*: "A chief of a Fulani clan in Nigeria dreamed that God said to him: 'What good will it be if you have the whole world but lose your place in heaven with Me?' When the chief told others about the dream and called for them to follow Jesus, almost 3,000 Fulani made decisions for Christ. While the new believers have encountered opposition from other traditionally Muslim Fulanis, they have maintained their determination to follow Jesus."

Spirit of Elijah Brings High Priest to Jesus

Writing in a prayer letter for S.W.A.T. ("Saints With A Target"), a ministry in Virginia Beach, Virginia, a verified source tells the following story about a field worker's visit to a village of the Madia tribe in India. A power encounter between the field worker and the village high priest proved life-changing for the influential priest and his family:

John (not his real name) had traveled many miles on foot with his two companions. Finally they reached the Madian village. Hot and thirsty, they asked for water, but the village people were afraid. Then, a village maiden brought them a drink. Suddenly, they heard a loud cry. A woman in a nearby hut was screaming. John asked, "Why is this woman in such distress?"

The maiden explained, "She is the wife of the village high priest and she is about to die. She's suffered much. Nothing has helped her." Immediately John and his friends went to see if they could pray for the woman.

They met with her husband, a greatly feared Madian priest. Devotees would travel many miles from three different states of India seeking his wisdom and blessings. The man had become rich through the people's offerings. His father and grandfather had also been priests in this same manner. Demonic signs and wonders kept a reverence alive in the hearts of the village people.

John sat across from the priest and asked, "If your wife gets healed when we pray for her in the Name of Jesus, will you give your heart to Him?" The priest replied, "Why do you bring this religion of foreigners into our village?" John explained, "Jesus is the Creator God and there is nothing foreign about Him. He is the God of the people."

The priest's stare was piercing. "I will keep you in place by the power of my demon spirits! You will not be able to move from the ground on which you sit! The whole village will witness that Jesus is not God!"

The priest went into a trance in order to conjure up the demon spirits to inhabit his body. John's companions were struck with fear and wanted to run, but John was steadfast. He prayed silently, binding the powers of darkness in Jesus' Name.

Meanwhile the whole village gathered to witness the spiritual showdown. Again and again the priest called upon the evil spirits. Suddenly he looked at John and said, "I don't understand! I can't get the evil spirits to take possession of me. What are you doing?" John simply explained that he was praying in the Name of Jesus against the evil spirits.

The priest was enraged and embarrassed. He picked up a burning log, ready to deal a crushing blow to John's head. As he raised it high, however, his arm froze in midair. No matter how hard he tried, he could not move it.

John removed the blazing log from the priest's hand and asked for permission to pray for his wife. The priest agreed. John and his two companions knelt in agonizing intercession for one and a half hours by the bed of the dying woman.

Suddenly she lifted her head and asked for water. Death had been denied. The priest heard the testimony of Jesus and renounced his Madian priesthood, forsaking his occupation and burning all of his idols and witchcraft objects. He and his dear wife have been walking with Jesus for six months now. John continues to disciple them in their new life with Christ.

Pray for Today's Leaders

The Nicodemuses of today's world need our prayers, whether they are open or hidden about their faith—indeed, whether they know the Lord yet or are allowing God to use them in a "Cyrus" role.

Some Nicodemuses cherish their positions and don't want to step out on the front lines, risking everything, unless they have complete assurance that what they are sensing is correct and of God. The Body of Christ can pray that they will have increased faith and confidence in the truth of the Gospel message. We can also pray against the fear of public opinion that would try to overtake them and ask God to give these leaders, in place of this fear, a reverent awe of Himself.

Many of these Nicodemuses, like the one who came to Jesus at night, need teaching, discipleship, mentoring, and encouraging in their faith. The Lord must give us both discernment to identify the hidden Nicodemuses and strategies to put mature believers into contact with these men and women.

A Christian with access to encourage and counsel the Nicodemus-like leaders of the world can have tremendous impact. Once a believer has gained the trust of such leaders, the believer can hold them accountable to fulfill the God-given mandates of their position. Mordecai, for instance, held Queen Esther accountable and encouraged her to fulfill her destiny as the only one with enough influence to speak to the king on behalf of the Jews: "Do not think that because you are in the king's house you alone of all the Jews will escape. For if you remain silent at this time, relief and deliverance for the Jews will arise from another place, but you and your father's family will perish. And who knows but that you have come to royal position for such a time as this?" (Esther 4:13-14). After three days of fasting, Esther summoned her courage to go before the king, where she successfully intervened on behalf of the Jews for their deliverance.

Scripture encouragingly tells us that God's hand remains on those leaders who are seeking truth and are willing to act in accordance with God's will. Although Nicodemus first came to Jesus at night, three years later he went boldly with Joseph of Arimathea during the day and stepped forward to declare that he was a disciple of the crucified Christ. May our risen Lord raise up many more men and women of influence to take a public stand for the Gospel in our day!

You Can Help Meet the Challenge

- Pray daily for those in positions of influence, that they would be used of God for His divine purpose for their lives.
- When God opens a door for you to speak to the Nicodemuses, ask Him for direction on how to approach them. What would open their eyes of understanding to accept Jesus?
- If you know Nicodemuses who are nominal Christians, pray for them and encourage them in the Lord. Ask the Holy Spirit to direct you in your relationship with them and to prepare you to disciple them into a deeper commitment to Christ.
- Pray that the Nicodemuses will allow God to use them to accomplish His purposes for their communities and societies.
- Christian expatriates are in excellent positions to be used by God to witness to Nicodemuses. Consider a bi-vocational position in one of the 10/40 Window countries.

Endnotes

1. Source: Name verified and withheld; reported in DAWN *Friday Fax* #12.98, 3 April 1998
2. Jane Rumph, *Stories from the Front Lines: Power Evangelism in Today's World*, Grand Rapids: Chosen Books, A Division of Baker Book House, 1996, pp. 229–230, used by permission
3. *The 10/40 Window Reporter*, Winter 1998, p. 3

7

The Great Spiritual Awakening in the 10/40 Window

*A*t the dawning of the 21st century, the fire of the Holy Spirit is breaking out again as in the 1st-century Church. This fresh blaze of God's Spirit is fanned by the praise and prayer of numerous believers from all over the world. The Holy Spirit is visiting the Church in its various nationalities, large and small assemblies, house churches, and traditional churches worldwide. Inspiring reports of God's power are flooding in from across the globe.

The Lord is multiplying His Church in an unprecedented way. In 1992 a missionary in Thailand spoke about the resistance of Thais to the Gospel. Now, only a few years later, the country is seeing a great harvest of souls. Hope of Bangkok Church, a single congregation pastored by a national believer in the capital city, now has 10,000 members!

Areas historically hostile to the Gospel now show remarkable church growth. In China, the number of Christians has exploded in the 50 years since the Communist takeover. India, historically resistant to the Gospel, is now home to an estimated 23 million believers.[1] Some evangelistic agencies suggest that

35,000 to 50,000 converts are being added to the Church daily in these two countries alone!

The Holy Spirit Is on the Move

Recent statistics verify unparalleled increases in church membership around the world, especially among evangelical, charismatic, and Pentecostal denominations. In a March 1998 report, "Global Trends and Mission, with a Special Focus on the 10/40 Window" (p. 5), I (Luis) quoted a review of the book *Megatrends 2000*, saying, "A 'global phenomenon' is taking place that will replace modernism and a reliance on science [for spiritual guidance]; 'the ideal of progress has given way to the return of faith.'"[2]

Across the 10/40 Window in particular, the Church has experienced amazing and explosive numerical growth over the past 50 years. Most of this growth has occurred during the 1990s, with the majority of this decade's increase coming in the latter half. In Kyrgyzstan, for instance, the first Kyrgyz came to Jesus in 1986, but today there may be nearly 4,000 Christian believers among them!

In Window nations once desolate of known believers, reports have emerged that the Holy Spirit is supernaturally birthing churches. One missionary referred to "church plants established by the Holy Spirit." For instance, believers in a church in a North African nation used to meet discreetly, fearing that non-believers would discover they had converted to Christianity. They carefully closed the doors and windows where they met, pulled the curtains, and worshiped quietly so their neighbors would not hear them. One day the church leader said that, as they were praying, the fear of what man could do to them left her. Instead she received the fear of the Lord. They then flung open the doors and curtains and began worshiping Jesus loudly. This leader said that the church decided not to hide any longer, because they have the light of God that their country needs and it must be proclaimed.

Another exciting development is the successful missions work of churches in Asia and Africa that are now dispatching teams into the 10/40 Window. An e-mail from a reliable source mentions the example of a small church in Singapore that sends people throughout China, Malaysia, India, Cambodia, and Vietnam.

The Holy Spirit is on the move, awakening lost souls to eternal life. This chapter features only a taste of the exciting work of God's grace erupting in country after country across the globe as churches awaken and grow exponentially. Come take a whirlwind tour around the world and rejoice at what the Holy Spirit is doing in the 10/40 Window today.

ALGERIA:
Gifts of the Holy Spirit Fuel Growth

In Algeria more than 400 Muslims became born again believers in a few months. In the midst of terrible circumstances, where fundamentalist Muslim groups still carry out brutal attacks even on women and children, the Christian Church is quietly growing. According to one of the country's Christian leaders, who can't be named here, one Christian group has grown from 800 to 1000 members since November 1996. All of the new members are Muslim Background Believers. According to eyewitnesses, the relatively quick growth is due to "increasing manifestations of the gifts of the Holy Spirit."[3]

BANGLADESH:
Workers Harvest Ripe Fields

Islam is the state religion of Bangladesh, and Muslim fundamentalists are eager to turn the nation into a strict Islamic state. The government, however, sees the work of Every Home Contact (EHC) as one that truly benefits many communities in Bangladesh because of its educational program and social-work projects. EHC workers have distributed more than 8,702,000 Gospel booklets, yielding a harvest of 219,420 responses and prompting the formation of 200 home fellowships. Thirty "houses of prayer" have also been established where as many as 115 believers come together in each home at least once a week for fasting and prayer.[4]

BURKINA FASO:
Churches Send Out National Missionaries

The AD2000 Movement office reports that "the days have passed in which the West alone is sending out missionaries. 'Mission from everywhere to everywhere' is the reality today. Burkina Faso's Jean Baptist Swadrago Church sends out 150 missionary couples each year, many of whom work in the almost unreached Sahel zone."[5]

CAMBODIA:
Cambodian Church Multiplies

A reliable source writes, "In an earlier letter I quoted a missionary...working in Cambodia who said that 'there is no other place like Cambodia within the 10/40 Window where there is such receptivity to the Gospel message.' I was able to meet with this brother and hear of the 40-plus churches that they have seen planted and the 25-plus preaching points where they hold evangelistic services (including one at the main temple, Wat Phnom). More recently I have received the report that a new church is organized in Cambodia every week among churches related to the Khmer Evangelical Church, which saw 13 congregations started in three months. [This group alone] has a goal of 300 new churches started by the year AD2000."[6]

Christians Bring Hope to the Nation

After many years of isolation and persecution, the Church in Cambodia is making significant strides. The state of Cambodia recognized and granted legal status to its Christian community in April 1990. As few as 10 small house churches represented Christ at that time. In 1995 approximately 300 churches in Cambodia were growing and multiplying. Observers attribute the growth to the fact that Christians bring hope to this country where the rule of law disintegrated during the political chaos of recent decades.[7]

CHINA:
China's "Back Door" Wide Open for the Gospel

China's revival may be the greatest since Jesus walked on the earth. Every day, an estimated 20,000 or more Chinese become Christians. In 1949, when Communism took over this nation, there were fewer than one million born-again believers after a full century of missionary work. Now there are 60 to 120 million or more, the majority of whom meet in unregistered house churches. Many Chinese evangelists, often teenage peasant girls, and even elderly people, are planting churches in unreached parts of their country.

Consider the "chance" encounter with a missionary that led to the founding of a fast-growing church in one of the least-evangelized areas of China. More than 500 people now are part of the fellowship, which traces its beginnings to an unexpected meeting five years ago between a Youth With A Mission (YWAM) worker and an elderly man.

The two met when the missionary was briefly visiting a village in the southwest part of China, home to approximately 15 million Zhuang—the largest of the country's many minority people groups. Unable to speak in a common language, the pair struck up "conversation" by writing in Chinese on a piece of paper. (All languages in China use the same written script.) The YWAM worker told the man about her faith, and he wrote that he wanted to become a Christian, too. They swapped addresses, and after she returned to her home in Hong Kong, the missionary received a letter asking her to return to tell him more about the Gospel.

When she went back several months later, she was surprised to find that the man had 11 friends with him, whom he had talked to about Christ. Going back again a few months later to help the new Christians grow in their faith, she discovered that the number had grown to about 30, as the first convert and his friends told others. By the time of her most recent visit, the Christians in the area—all Zhuang, traditionally Buddhist-animist—numbered more than 500, and had formed themselves into a church, with the man with whom the missionary had her initial contact appointed as one of the leaders.[8]

ETHIOPIA:
One of the Great Missionary Forces

Not many years ago, Christian churches were underground in the ex-Communist country of Ethiopia. Now the Church is not only out in the open, but has grown exponentially. The Ethiopian Church could well become one of the great missionary forces at the turn of the millennium. The evangelical body has now grown to a million believers and revival has been ignited in the Orthodox Church. It is estimated that 200,000 believers have come to a personal faith in Jesus Christ.[9]

INDIA:
Signs of Spiritual Breakthrough

North India stands at a unique moment in its history; the Holy Spirit is moving in this area as perhaps never before. In the past 25 years, just nine organizations have started over 5,680 churches and preaching centers. If church planting is an indicator of incipient revival, the figures below are very encouraging:

India Evangelical Team—700 churches; India Evangelical Mission—more than 400 churches; Friends Missionary Prayer Band—more than 400 churches; the Evangelical Church of India—more than 400 churches; Bible Christian Mission (BCM)—more than 312 congregations and more than 1,500 preaching centers; Rajasthan Bible Institute—more than 600 churches and prayer groups; Gospel for Asia—750 churches; Filadelphia Fellowship—550 churches; Vishwa Vani—80 churches. This is but a sampling of what God has done in recent years in building His Church in North India; the many independent churches and small denominations and mission agencies are not included in these figures.

According to Bihar state's mission researcher S. D. Ponraj, in his recent book *The Tribal Challenge,* a large part of the revival has occurred within tribes that are very open to the Gospel. In

Bihar 34,000 people from the Maltos and Santhalis tribes have been baptized in the last decade and now meet in 375 churches and groups. A growing number of Indian networks and groups see a "kairos" moment in God's plan for North India that must not be missed and are making appropriate plans. "World Reach," the missionary section of the Christian Broadcasting Network (CBN) in Virginia Beach, Virginia, and Newlife Fellowship Churches, a network of more than 1,200 house churches in Bombay (now Mumbai), have started a strategic cooperation to reach 500 million people through evangelistic direct mail and a personal follow-up within six weeks of the mailing. The group expects 65 million decisions by the year 2000.[10]

From Military Cook to Preacher of the Gospel

An ordinary military cook watched one of India's many healing preachers and thought to himself, "What he can do, I can do, too." He now holds services, in Jesus' Name, every Sunday from 9 a.m. to 5 p.m. in a large tent in the countryside. He offers an all-around service from which people can choose like a buffet. He preaches, teaches, prays for the sick, and drives out demons, and the people can come and go as they please. It fits in well with the Indian village culture; it is impossible to arrive too late because there is no official start or end. Many Hindus come, listen for a while, leave to fetch some friends, return, leave again, and drop in again at the end.

The "Indian-style church for the unchurched" regularly has an attendance of between 400 and 500. The ex-cook deals with demons quickly, saying "'Oh, a demon! Down on your knees—don't even dare to stand in the presence of a servant of God. Come and crawl before me!' Then he prays in Jesus' Name and the person is set free...."[11]

Rescued from the Sacrificial Altar

Lalit from Orissa state was, as he describes himself, "a worldly singer" before contracting a fatal illness. He lay on his death bed for three months before seeing a vision of Jesus.

"Jesus was carrying something like a rod in His hand, and touched me on my bed. I was healed. I have been serving Him since then!" he says.

To start with, Lalit became a preacher and tract-distributor with Every Home for Christ. One day, his leader sent him with a small team to distribute tracts near Kulpani, which Lalit describes as having many fanatical Hindus. One of the villages to which they were sent was infamous for its Kali-Mandal, a temple to the goddess Kali, to whom human sacrifices are still made today. Lalit hadn't been there long when people started warning him, "Babapriest, the head priest, is already searching for you. They want to sacrifice you to Kali. Run away quickly!" Too late—500 armed men captured the small team, beat them, and dragged them to the Kali temple, where the priest was waiting with a large sword. "Deny Jesus and turn to Kali, or Kali will drink your blood today!" They gave Lalit cow dung mixed with water to drink, but he said to his Lord, "If I die, I am with You. If I live, I will continue to serve You. My life is in Your hand."

The priest lifted his sword, but was interrupted by a woman shouting, "Let him go. We don't want to see that any more." Other women took up the cry, and Lalit was able to escape.

Today, he is a modern David. When he plays his flute (the "rod" he saw in Jesus' hand in his vision), people are healed and demons driven out. He and his team of 25 have planted 110 churches since 1992 and have baptized almost 3,000 people. Lalit says, "There are now three churches with a total of some 150 members in the Kali-Mandal village."[12]

Revival in Madhya Pradesh

One of the most amazing church movements in India at the moment is in Madhya Pradesh, a state in central India. According to reports from Dr. Victor Choudhrie, former medical director of the Christian Medical College in Ludhiana, the number of Bible schools in the almost unreached state grew from four to 14 during the first years of *Praying Through The Window,* 1993–1997. The number of churches has grown from

500 to more than 1,000 in the last four years, a growth rate of around 16 percent per year, even greater than the current 13 percent growth rate in Madras (now Chennai).

Dr. Choudhrie attributes the growth to a new vision among the Christians for cooperative evangelization, and efforts to gather 1,000 regular intercessors from all over India for each of the state's districts as well as another 1,000 intercessors from all over the world. An increasing number of Christians in Madhya Pradesh have been forming a network since 1993. Their goal is to plant a church in each village and part of town in the state's 45 districts. Within this region, there are 66,000 villages and 66 million inhabitants. If the current developments continue, the number of churches will grow exponentially to reach 100,000 in the next 30 years.[13]

IRAQ:
Church Growth in Basra

The missions organization Open Doors reports that the Evangelical Church in Basra, Iraq, which a few years ago consisted of only two families meeting in a dilapidated facility, now incorporates 60 families. They were able to build a new church building in a convenient area of the city, partly with government assistance. In a cooperative effort, Open Doors and the Bible Society of Jordan delivered over thirty-six tons of Bibles and books to Baghdad in the spring of 1996. The Bible was the most-requested book at the fair! A known thirty-seven Iraqis are currently enrolled in an evangelical seminary in the Middle East. Praise God for this dramatic advance for the Gospel among Iraqi Arabs![14]

MONGOLIA:
Villagers Make Trek to Request Church Planter

Not long ago, some strangely dressed people burst into a Christian meeting in the Mongolian capital, Ulan Bator. They had arrived from the Gobi Altai, a region largely unreached by the Gospel. After viewing the *JESUS* film, these strange visitors had been meeting in one of the village leader's houses to read the Bible. The purpose of their long journey was to inquire, "When can someone come to start a church?"[15]

MOROCCO:
Spiritual Climate Dramatically Improves

A church in the United States sent a team on a prayer journey to Morocco in October 1997. In the prayer journey report, a team member writes:

"On Sunday we were blessed to be able to attend a small expatriate church. The majority of the choir is comprised of Middle Eastern and South African students. Additionally, on the day we visited, the service was led by two Mexican women who were there ministering to French-speaking Moroccan women.

"Our visit was significant in that, since visiting Morocco two-and-a-half years earlier, we sensed that the spiritual climate had improved dramatically. The workers confirmed that this is the case, and that over the past few years the spiritual climate throughout most of the nation has become stronger. People are now more receptive and tolerant of the teachings of Christ. The workers attribute this predominantly to two factors: (1) the amount of prayer that has been offered over the 10/40 Window in the course of the past six years and (2) the four hours daily of Christian broadcasting that comes into the country via satellite dishes."

The church sending this team has adopted a specific Moroccan people group and has one couple in final preparation to go to Morocco to learn the language and eventually to plant a church among the Central Shilha Berbers.[16]

MYANMAR:
Great Advances for the Gospel after Prayer Journey

A Myanmar (Burma) prayer journeyer writes:

"The second trip in April of 1998 showed that many of those who lacked excitement in their walk with the Lord eight months earlier were now greatly encouraged. The joy of the Lord has been loosed in many churches, and hope has been established. Good reports are coming in of areas opening up to the Gospel, people being raised from the dead, sick being healed, and people movements happening. Several church planters have reported healings. Some report Buddhists seeing visions and being healed and turning to Christ. One church I visited had more than doubled in size in nine months, and not all could even fit inside the small house church. One evangelist told of leading 20 Hindu tribal people to Christ. These were Hindu men who had worshiped by puncturing their chests and tongues and dancing on hot coals. I worshiped with these men, and the joy to be set free in Jesus was something to behold. Their children and wives also worshiped the true God with great joy!"[17]

NEPAL:
Explosive Growth of the Kingdom

In 1997 it was reported that in three years, the number of churches in Kathmandu, Nepal, has jumped from 23 to 85. One congregation, which began in the back room of a book shop, has grown to more than 2,000 members. During an evangelistic effort, the Gospel was shared with 1,200 Nepalis, and 400 made decisions for Christ. Praise God for the explosive growth of the kingdom in Nepal. Ask God to draw thousands more to Himself before the end of the year. Pray for the effective witness of Nepali believers.[18]

700 Come to Christ in One Month

Shortly after returning from a prayer journey to Nepal, Lori, an intercessor, received the following letter:

"I would like to thank you for coming to our country to pray for our people. May God reward you all for that. Things have changed since you left, especially among the Tharus, our targeted people group. They are open to the Gospel now. I believe it is because of your prayers. The month of November [1997] was very significant for us. More than 700 people received Jesus as their Lord and Savior, and several thousand people had the opportunity to hear the Gospel in far west Nepal. We praise God and give Him all the glory."[19]

VIETNAM:
"Barbed-Wire Christians" Return

In the late 1970s, literally hundreds of thousands of people fled Vietnam in leaky boats only to be interned in refugee camps in Hong Kong and elsewhere. Among the over 53,000 Vietnamese refugees being repatriated from camps in Hong Kong are hundreds of "barbed-wire Christians"—so called because they converted to the Christian faith in prison-like holding camps. In an otherwise sad story, a missionary worker in the camps told Compass Direct, "The exciting thing is that, since 1988, most Vietnamese refugees came from northern Vietnam, so these new Christians are going home to a part of Vietnam that has traditionally been very resistant to the Gospel." In the north of Vietnam, there are few churches and pastors to nourish Christians in the faith—a stark contrast to southern Vietnam, where the bulk of the country's more than 500,000 Protestants live and worship.[20]

You Can Help Meet the Challenge

- Praise God for the wonderful spiritual awakening among the peoples of the 10/40 Window.
- Continue to pray daily for more breakthroughs among unreached people groups.
- Circulate widely stories of how the Holy Spirit is moving to save the lost in order to encourage intercessors that their prayers are being answered.
- Consider how to support Christian ministries working where the fields are white for harvest.
- Find out if there are international students from the 10/40 Window in your city by contacting ministries that work with them, including International Students, Inc. and Campus Crusade for Christ.
- Find out if refugees have resettled in your area, or if your workplace employs or hosts internationals. Pray for open doors and open hearts as you prayerwalk campuses, neigh-

borhoods, and businesses in places that have a high concentration of 10/40 Window peoples.
- Pray for believers in 10/40 Window countries to remain steadfast in faith despite persecution. Ask God to give strategies for church planting in difficult areas.
- Contact Christian Information Network to find out how to participate in a prayer journey and witness firsthand demonstrations of the Holy Spirit's power.

Endnotes

1. Source: U.S. State Department report on India, July 1997 estimates.
2. Quoted by Jay Rogers in his review, "Megatrends authors predict spiritual awakening for the 1990s," in *The Forerunner,* September 1990; reprinted by permission from Media House International, Melbourne, Florida. *Megatrends 2000,* by John Naisbitt and Patricia Aburdene, William Morrow, 1990
3. Source: Name verified and withheld; reported in DAWN Friday Fax #18.97, 9 May 1997
4. Source: Every Home for Christ, e-mail sent 17 December 1998
5. Source: AD2000 Movement office, fax sent 3 April 1997
6. Source: Name verified and withheld
7. Source: MARC newsletter, December 1996; reported by Brigada, 6 February 1997
8. Source: YWAM News Digest, 3 April 1997
9. Source: Neil Anderson, The Sowers Ministry, "Report on Horn of Africa Prayer Initiative, 15–19 February 1998"
10. Source: Dr. Raju Abraham, D. S. Ponraj; Mission Educational Books, Bihar; reported in DAWN Friday Fax #18.97, 9 May 1997
11. Source: Dr. Victor Choudhrie, Betul, Madhya Pradesh; reported in DAWN Friday Fax #49.97, 19 December 1997
12. Source: Lalit Kumar Nayak, Phulbani, Orissa; reported in DAWN Friday Fax #49.97, 19 December 1997
13. Source: Dr. Victor Choudhrie, Betul, Madhya Pradesh; reported in DAWN Friday Fax #7.97, 21 February 1997
14. Source: Open doors August 1996 newsletter; reported in DAWN Friday Fax #35.96, 6 September 1996, additional sources, verified and withheld.

15. Source: Global Glimpse; reported in DAWN Friday Fax #49.96, December 1996
16. Source: Name verified and withheld; prayer journey report
17. Source: Name verified and withheld; church in Woodland Park, Colorado; prayer journey report, April 1998, p. 2
18. Source: *Advance* newsletter, June 1997, advance-newsletter@xc.org
19. Source: Name verified and withheld; reported in *The 10/40 Window Reporter*, Spring 1998, p. 9
20. Source: Compass Direct; reported by Brigada, 15 May 1997

8

Jerusalem, God's Beloved

*P*edestrians strolled down the tree-lined avenue, less than an hour's commute from Jerusalem, enjoying the beautiful day in Tel Aviv. Suddenly, the tranquil scene was shattered by a powerful explosion. Bodies slammed against buildings. Body parts were propelled into trees. Blood splattered everywhere. Horror registered on every face. A lone suicide bomber had unleashed this carnage.

As people realized the enormity of what had taken place, the wailing began. In accordance with Orthodox Jewish tradition, workers arriving at the scene quickly and methodically removed every trace of human remains. Even the human blood was meticulously washed from the streets and buildings.

Not long after the bombing occurred, a group of intercessors visited the site. As they prayed and walked on the street, they found it difficult to comprehend the carnage. Why was the bomb detonated? What possible reason could there be to inflict such pain, misery, and death on innocent adults and defenseless children?

One motive of terrorism is revenge, fueled by *hate*—the kind of hate that has existed for thousands of years in the Middle East. This enmity exists between two peoples, the Arabs and the Jews—relatives, really. It's a family feud that dates back to the time of Sarah and Hagar in the first book of the Old Testament. Two of Abraham's sons, Ishmael and Isaac, played in the desert sands together as children—after all, they were brothers. But jealousy and competition arose between Hagar, Ishmael's mother, and Sarah, Isaac's mother. Over the centuries the animosity between the descendants of these two sons of Abraham has intensified.

Terrorism in Israel is not limited to Arabs against Jews. It was reported in *The Guardian* newspaper that a Jewish man, dressed in ultra-Orthodox Jewish clothing, has stalked and attacked Palestinians. In a recent incident, presumably the same man, whom authorities suspect in previous murders, stabbed and killed a Palestinian father of six who worked for the city of Jerusalem.[1] Clearly, only God's love, freely given through His Son Jesus, can bring reconciliation between these warring peoples.

In 1993, two years prior to this bombing, I (Beverly) traveled to Israel for the first time. Joining me on her second trip to Israel was Wanda Elliott, my best friend and prayer partner. Our intercessory prayer journey team of two arrived in Israel just three weeks after the Lord called upon us to make the trip. Tucked carefully into our baggage were the names of the members of our church, to be prayed over while we were in Israel. Our precious cargo also contained prayer requests from friends and family to be placed in the over-stuffed cracks of the Western, or "Wailing," Wall of the Temple in Jerusalem.

While in Israel, we would take part in *Praying Through The Window I* and also meet David Russett, our intercessor friend who had already been in the land for two months praying for the Jewish people. God had given Wanda and me specific orders to pray for the "brothers," meaning the Jews and the Arabs.

Our plans called for us to stay in East Jerusalem. But even before our arrival, David expressed concern about us lodging in that area because of spontaneous fighting that had erupted earlier. After an initial meeting, David took us to our first Shabbat meal. After our lovely meal, our driver, Beth, escorted us to the location in East Jerusalem where we would be based for our 10 days of prayer. David still felt uncomfortable about the situation, but he agreed to accompany us anyway. Wanda rode with David, and I rode with Beth.

On the way, I asked Beth to stop at a small neighborhood store so I could buy some bottled water. As we exited the shop, I looked over at David and Wanda and saw looks of terror on their faces. Feeling safe, I didn't understand why they were so concerned.

When we arrived at the place where we were to stay, David's trepidation intensified. He didn't want to leave us there. We decided to pray. I'll never forget the glory of the Lord filling that place as we worshiped and prayed together. That night the Holy Spirit took away all of our anxiety about being in a volatile area.

Our days and nights passed in intercession over Jerusalem. Every morning we were awakened by the Islamic call to prayer and roosters crowing. Both of these sounds were chilling, but the cockcrows sobered us, reminding us daily of Peter's denial of Christ.

Our main prayer focus for Israel centered on interceding for God to reveal Himself to the people living in the land and for Him to pour out His grace on the Messianic congregations meeting in Yeshua's Name. We also prayed that God would raise up strong leadership in these assemblies to evangelize Israel.

God used this and other prayer journeys to give us an increased understanding of His work in Israel and the Middle East. He has chosen to establish His Name among the Jewish people. His faithfulness and love for the Jews is evident in Israel. As we prayed, we felt strongly that the physical and spiritual restoration of the Jews is directly tied to the fulfillment of the Great Commission. According to Romans 11:25-26, when the full number of Gentiles has been added to the Church, then all Israel will be saved. God is a covenant-keeping God. He will keep His promises to Israel. Christ must stir the Jews to jealousy first by reflecting in the Gentiles the life, power, purity, and presence of the Holy One of Israel.

Every year thousands of believers visit Israel, taking tours and attending conferences. Sadly, most believers coming to the Holy Land are interested only in "dead stones"—the centuries-old biblical and historical sites. Many never visit or fellowship with the "living stones"—those believers living, working, and struggling to survive in an inhospitable place.

Any trip to Israel is a wonderful opportunity to pray for and support the local believers—Jews, Palestinians, and Arabs. Visiting Christians can fellowship with the brothers and sisters there, who are members of the Body of Christ; they can take time to learn what their needs are so these resident believers can be strengthened to continue the work God has called them to do in the land. The believers in Israel will be encouraged when the rest of us throughout His kingdom do not ignore them but rather embrace them as brothers and sisters in the Lord.

Arab Muslim Background Believers (MBBs) living in Israel and the West Bank feel particularly left out when Christians come from all over the world and don't fellowship with them. In fact, many Western believers are shocked to learn that Arab believers exist! In *Operation World*, editor Patrick Johnstone states that Palestine was 30 percent Christian in 1940 (p. 314). Ongoing conflict with their Arab brothers who are Muslims and political and economic conditions have driven many Arab believers to emigrate. Only 2.5 percent of the remaining Arabs were believers in 1990 (p. 315). Yet significant numbers of Arab minorities who follow Christ still exist in such towns as Nazareth and Bethlehem.

Although the number of believers in these towns has decreased, God is moving in marvelous ways to promote the Gospel. At the Palestinian Bible College in Bethlehem, men and women train for full-time ministry among their people. The city of Jesus' birth is the headquarters of a Christian radio and television station that has been approved by the Palestinian

Authority. The Palestinian Authority has also recently given permission to believers to distribute Bibles, devotionals, and audio and video cassettes during the Christmas Eve services held in Manger Square. These gifts, provided by the local and international church, were mostly distributed to Muslims.

A growing number of Muslims are requesting the Bible and other instructional material. Many of them are responding to the message of new life in Jesus.[2]

Religion amid Secular Culture

The holiest day in the Jewish liturgical calendar is the Day of Atonement. This day, called Yom Kippur, comes in late September or early October at the end of a ten-day period marked by fasting. More than 70 percent of Israel fasts on Yom Kippur.

Despite widespread observance of Yom Kippur, there is a spiritual void in Israel. Large numbers of Jews live secular lives, similar to nominal Christians in the United States who attend church only on Easter Sunday. People who have assimilated aspects of the secular culture, particularly young people, try to fill their spiritual vacuum with idols of materialism and humanism. Immoral practices have infiltrated society. As a result, Israel has one of the highest abortion rates in the world. Tragically, about one third of all pregnancies in Israel are terminated. Pray that Israel's eyes will be opened to this silent death and that more Jews would honor the timeless truths of the God of Israel.

For intercessors, the Day of Atonement represents an excellent opportunity to pray for the conviction of sin, for the spirit of repentance, and for grace and supplication to come upon the Jewish people. The Lord ordained the Day of Atonement in Leviticus 16. At this annual solemn ceremony, the High Priest presented to God the blood of a sin offering to cleanse himself and the people of Israel from all their sins of the previous year. Now Jews around the world typically spend Yom Kippur at their local synagogue in confession of sin and pursuit of forgiveness. We should pray that the goodness of God would lead them to true repentance and the knowledge of their Messiah. He is the only One who can give them the peace they so desperately seek and need. His Blood made atonement for their sins once and for all.

Love Conquers Hate

A Christian Arab leader tenderly tells the story of how God placed love in his heart for the Jewish people in the land.

"From the area of Moab my father came, and from the heights of Gilead my mother came. In Jerusalem I was born, on the Via Dolorosa—on a mission field. The surroundings were a bit strange—a Jordanian family among a Palestinian majority, a Christian among a Muslim majority and an evangelical among a traditional Christian majority. And on top of this, another factor came into the picture: war in 1967, with masses of soldiers, dead bodies in the streets of Jerusalem, people hiding underground. Suddenly we were under the military rule of another strange presence—the Israeli army. I remember my father going out near the end of the fighting to look for his brother, a Jordanian soldier, among the dead bodies in the streets.

"This is the background of my childhood, and around me existed every reason to fill my heart with fear, hatred, discrimination, and a desire to be insulated and protected from everything outside my own family. Yet my father, a pastor, was spiritually awake enough not to fall victim to the tyranny of the political and social situation. He chose the way of the cross, the road of divine love. He established in me and in my brothers' and sisters' lives, through a rich impartation of the Scriptures, a strong foundation which could stand the tremendous pressure from the outside—the pressure of the way of the world, the cycle of violence, killing, hatred, and injustice. As long as I live, I will always owe this [debt of gratitude] to my parents.

"After leaving home to attend university in Iraq from 1981 to 1985, I found myself again in a war situation—a bloody war between Iraq and Iran. At that time most of the world was standing on the side of Iraq against the 'frightening Khomeini monster.' Every day on the TV we listened to highly charged nationalistic and wartime songs—every day we were subjected to scenes of dead and burned Iranian soldiers. The whole atmosphere shouted, 'These people are Muslim fanatics; they are the worst enemy,' thus exhorting me to rejoice over every defeat the Iranians would suffer.

"In this experience Satan attempted to kill in me the divine love for human beings created after the image of my Father. Every day I had to go back to Calvary to receive healing and forgiveness. I needed this daily trip 'far from the madding crowd' to go into seclusion with my heavenly Father and regain the outlook of Christ. I was protected in the palm of His hand.

"Returning to Jordan for further studies, I had opportunity to reflect. By that time the Lord's calling became very clear in my life: He wanted me to go and serve Him in the Holy Land among the Muslim Palestinians. I realized then the reason for the road along which the Lord had led me all of the previous years: He needed to deliver me from all traces of hatred and prejudice, to impart His Love in me, so that I could gain His divine outlook and perspective. Ask and you shall be given, the Scriptures say: I asked the Lord to fill me with His love for Iranians, for Palestinians, for Muslims of all kinds, so that I might love with His love everybody who is created after His image—all my relatives and neighbors.

"Moreover, I asked the Lord to fill me with His love for the Jewish people because I was going to serve Him among the Palestinian people! To serve the Lord among the Serbs you need to ask for God's love for the Croatians. To serve the Lord among any people group, you should have—in addition to love for the group itself—God's love for the worst enemy of this group, because there is no way to serve if I do not love. For me to be able to minister reconciliation and liberty and forgiveness, the Lord had to create these as realities in my life. To do so, He exposed me to a number of human conflicts to help me see that by the end of the day all of these conflicts are tools in the hand of Satan to kill and destroy more.

"As the Lord gave me His love for the Jewish people, I realized that this love is not based on a certain doctrinal position regarding Israel and the End Times. Nor is it based on a foundation of guilt from the past, or a reactionary love to express my support for them because they stand against Muslim fundamentalists. It is simply God's basic love for humanity, the love that knows no discrimination—the love of the cross."[3]

Reconciliation—the Key to Life

These are tumultuous times in the Holy Land and the Middle East. Yet God continues to work in many ways in the midst of the turmoil. Veteran missionary Ray Register has documented the extraordinary advance of church-planting efforts in both Israel and the Palestinian territories.

Despite overwhelming obstacles and highly complex issues facing the church-planting effort, the last 20 years have seen remarkable responsiveness and spiritual advancement in these ancient lands. In the past five years, a minimum of 200 Arab Muslims have become believers in Christ and assemble in mobile congregations. These new believers are affectionately referred to as Muslim Background Believers (MBBs). According to Ray Register, the number of Messianic Jewish house churches and congregations has multiplied from fewer than ten 25 years ago, to more than 100 today.

Because of Israeli occupation of the West Bank since 1967, serious tensions have arisen between Palestinian believers and Messianic Jews. The relationship between them is very complex. Palestinian, Arab, and Israeli children live in an environment of suspicion, with pervasive insinuations that people of the "other" culture can't be trusted. Friendships among these people groups are difficult to cultivate and even harder to maintain. For decades, a towering wall of challenges has impeded their path to reconciliation. Past experiences of interaction tended to be negative. Encounters often ended in arguments about whose view of Israel was correct. Currently, however, a concerted effort is underway to make the fellowship between these communities less strained.

For the sake of reconciliation, some believers are willing to risk being ridiculed and worse. A Palestinian believer may try to engage a Jewish man in conversation. A Messianic believer may attempt to befriend a Muslim. Each defies the cultural taboos. Skepticism pervades everyday relationships when interaction between cultures occurs. The risk-takers face likely ostracism from their friends, colleagues, peers, and families. They may be branded as traitors, shunned, or persecuted. They may even suffer physically, financially, or emotionally because they have taken a small step towards eliminating the walls dividing their society.[4]

The Need for Musalaha in the Land

Musalaha is the Arabic word for reconciliation and forgiveness. It is also the name of an organization of Messianic and Arabic believers who are striving to end years of isolation between the two fractured groups. They not only dialogue but also worship and take communion together. For most participants, the experience of worshiping and fellowshiping with someone outside of their own Christian circle can prove unnerving.

Part of Musalaha's strategy to bring the two sides together involves going beyond a limited time of worship. Messianic, Palestinian, and Arab believers take extended "camping trips" to the Negev. To survive in the desert requires teamwork, and there is no escape once they have arrived. The director of the program, Salim Munayer, states, "It's not Jewish, it's not Palestinian, it's not a classroom or a church. We're stuck out there; we can't run away." He further comments, "It's like putting a man in a microwave. We've seen people come with really extreme political opinions, and after one day in the desert, there's a real change, a visible openness. It's amazing: You throw them in the desert, and something happens."

What usually "happens" is that people are forced to trust one another, to cooperate for survival. Each team of two is given a camel. One rides while the other walks, and then they switch. The message that Musalaha is trying to communicate by these exercises is that we need each other. Solid friendships have been formed through this experience. Not only do the participants bond, but their families often welcome the "outsider" into their lives and hearts.[5]

Walls of Division Broken

Further indications that God is bringing the Body of Christ into greater unity were evident in February 1996 during the Jerusalem 2000 Celebration. At the Solemn Assembly at Jerusalem's YMCA, pastors and leaders of the Messianic Jewish and Arabic churches gathered together. Plans included a time of prayer to bring reconciliation through repentance and giving and receiving forgiveness, regardless of the opposing doctrinal views held by those who met together.

Jesus prayed for the unity of all believers in John 17. It is not the will of God that His Son's Bride is divided or that distrust should reign. Ephesians 2:14 says, "For he himself is our peace, who has made the two one and has destroyed the barrier, the dividing wall of hostility." Only the power of the miracle-working Spirit of God could bring together church leadership of two divided peoples living in one nation, people who are at times in sharp disagreement over territorial rights and religious issues.

The Solemn Assembly also provided an opportunity for reconciliation between local and visiting believers. One of the primary concerns discussed at the Solemn Assembly was that organizers of major international events hosted by visiting believers in Israel tend to ignore the local church bodies there. In fact, these conferences with their worldwide participation often divide resident believers and cause strife and confusion. Since the local Body of Christ is the spiritual gatekeeper of Jerusalem, this oversight by those coming to the city and to Israel in general is a significant problem.

Participants in the Solemn Assembly included Dr. C. Peter Wagner, coordinator of the United Prayer Track of the AD2000 Movement, and his wife, Doris, and Pastor Bob Beckett of Hemet, California. Those of us present at the Assembly witnessed a major breakthrough in the Spirit. Dr. Wagner and Pastor Beckett stood up to represent the leadership of the Body of Christ. They asked forgiveness from all present for violating and not honoring the host church of Jerusalem. Afterwards two brothers, one Jewish and the other Arab, were called to the front where Dr. Wagner and Pastor Beckett washed the two brothers' feet.

Dr. Wagner began to replace the socks of the Jewish brother. As he did, the Arab believer stopped him. The Arab then began to wash the feet of his Jewish brother. Tears began flowing. The Jewish man in turn washed his Arab brother's feet. Walls of animosity crumbled. Healing between those two members of the Body of Messiah began on that day. During this atmosphere of restoration, a Messianic leader came forward and washed Dr. Wagner's feet, blessing him for being a leader who would come and represent the Body so that healing could begin.[6]

Intercession for Complex Issues

After this tremendous example of humility and forgiveness, Solemn Assembly participants went to several of the high places in Jerusalem to intercede and bless the city as the Body of Christ together. Jesus told us in John 10:10 that Satan's purpose is to steal, kill, and destroy; the enemy of God can't stand the unity of the Body.

Shortly after the Solemn Assembly, terrorist attacks took place. The devil, pressed against the wall, seemingly tried to retaliate for the spiritual breakthrough. The only answer to the turmoil that has tormented Israel in the past and still plagues the land today is supernatural intervention. When the enemy comes in like a flood, God will lift up a banner to proclaim His purpose and intent (Isa. 59:19, KJV). The uniting of the Body of Christ in Israel has significant implications. Many see this as the beginning of a worldwide move of reconciliation among all believers.

Continued prayer will prove crucial in order to deal with the variety of issues that have kept Palestinian and Jewish believers separated. None is more divisive than the debate over the land. Two main perspectives fuel the heated discussions between the two sides: Jewish believers' concern centers mostly on who owns the land, while Arab believers' concern centers on their people's economic and political viability. These ongoing questions need to be settled.

In 1999, a Jerusalem II council will meet. Messianic and Gentile congregations in Israel will attempt to reconcile these and other differences. Through open dialogue and prayer, planners hope the Spirit will resolve this conflict. Believers around the world are needed to intercede on a massive scale before, during, and after this meeting. Without divine intervention on behalf of Israel, the Palestinian territories, and the people who live in the land, growing conflict could erupt in unparalleled violence. The issues are extremely complex. There are no simple solutions to a problem that has existed for thousands of years. Pray that the power of the Holy Spirit will sweep the region, bringing revival to the Church and repentance to all inhabitants of the Holy Land.[7]

Finally, we must keep in mind that there are a growing number of believers among the Muslim population. In order for true reconciliation to take root, develop, and blossom, these new MBBs must be included in any move in that direction. *All* believers in the Holy Land must be considered vital elements and participants regarding reconciliation.[8]

The Battle to Curtail Religious Freedom

Despite some marvelous moves of God in the region, believers still face enormous pressure from many segments of society. In December 1997 a bill was introduced in the Knesset, Israel's parliament, to restrict evangelism. This bill aimed to make it illegal to possess or distribute literature or speak of one's faith with intent to encourage another to "change religions." Ultra-orthodox Jews oppose the free-speech rights of evangelicals to share the Gospel with their neighbors.

After international protest, the bill's sponsors backed down considerably. But within three weeks, a second bill, even more punitive, was introduced in response to the weakening of the original measure. This one, too, would put significant obstacles in the way of evangelism. It passed its preliminary reading by vote of the entire cabinet, including Prime Minister Benjamin Netanyahu—despite the Prime Minister's assurances amid the controversy over the earlier bill that his government would oppose such legislation.[9]

During an interview at Christian Information Network, a Messianic believer from Israel stated that the measure would carry punishment in the form of fines from US $13,000 to $15,000 and imprisonment of up to three years. As of the fall of 1998, the bill is still being debated and must pass three committees before it becomes law.

This Messianic believer also shared that some of the local believers have been harassed. Their pictures have been posted around the neighborhood where they live, with captions reading, "These people are out to steal your souls." Believers have received late night phone calls from people making veiled threats. The Hebrew press has actively bashed Messianic Jews, asserting that they are part of a cult. In some places of Israeli society, Messianic Jews are not welcomed. Often employers will deny a promotion if they find out that the person in line for advancement is a messianic believer. Tensions run high between believers and those who want to curtail the freedom to openly declare Jesus as the Messiah.[10]

Messianic believers are not the only ones under fire. Arab MBBs have been persecuted and tortured under the governance of the Palestinian Authority—by the Palestinian Preventative Security Services—for their faith in Jesus Christ. A media watch group in Israel has investigated and substantiated the validity of allegations made by Arab MBBs who have suffered for their faith. Amnesty International also has evidence of these occurrences. It is not easy for Arab MBBs to live in their communities, where the predominant religion is hostile to their beliefs.

Israeli television recently broadcast a special on the growing number of incidents involving persecution of Arab MBBs by Muslims. A legal advisor for the Palestinian Authority said that former Muslims who believe in Jesus as Christ and do not return to their religion are violating the tenets of Islam and run the risk of execution. The Islamic Sharee'ah says that converts to another religion should be executed: "…The punishment for apostasy (riddah) is well known in Islamic Sharee'ah. The one who leaves Islam will be asked to repent by the Sharee'ah judge in an Islamic country; if he does not repent and come back to 'the true religion,' he will be killed as a kaafir [unbeliever] and apostate, because of the command of the Prophet…: 'Whoever changes his religion, kill him.'"[11]

So far there are no reports of any executions taking place in Israel.[12]

Satan's Strategies in Jerusalem and the Middle East

God has a plan and a vision for Israel. But the devil also has a plan and a vision for what he wants to accomplish in the land. He is waging spiritual warfare against the nation of Israel and trying to undermine and thwart the plan of God in the region.

Satan uses several ploys to combat the purposes of God. He deceives believers to follow another gospel (Gal. 1:8-9). He lures believers into a lukewarm relationship with their Lord, enticing them to chase after the things of this world. He also attempts to keep people from God by bombarding them with a "spirit of rejection." God's heart is toward the nation of Israel. But Satan blinds the eyes of the Jews to keep them from accepting their Messiah. God's enemy knows that if he can cause them to continue to reject Jesus, he will have accomplished his work. Believers committed to sharing the Gospel with the Jewish people often feel discouraged because of the hardness of hearts they encounter.

Delusion, depression, and deception are other methods Satan employs to counter God's intentions for the inhabitants of Israel. If the adversary can disable vessels prepared as temples of the Holy Spirit and make them ineffective, then his tactics will succeed.

The antagonism between Christian believers and the Muslim Arab world is another device used by the Prince of Darkness in warfare against God's plan. A war is being waged on earth and in the heavenlies. For believers to triumph in the midst of this spiritual battle, we must lay aside politics and cultural intolerance, focusing on one great theme: reaching the world with the Gospel.

Messianic Jews and Arab MBBs have started to realize they are one in Christ. This awareness began to grow after the *intifada*, the Palestinian uprising that took place during the 1980s. During the early 1990s, a solid move toward reconciliation between all believers began to take hold in Israel. Some Arab believers worship in Messianic Jewish congregations in Israel. They are among a group of courageous men and women actively tearing down barriers that have kept the communities apart. No doubt there have been injuries—physical, emotional, and spiritual—on all sides. All involved need to extend forgiveness for these wounds. If either Jews or Arabs hold onto the atrocities committed against them throughout history by those acting in the Name of Christ, it will be difficult for them to accept the message of Jesus and His followers. The reality of who Jesus Christ is and what He stands for far outweighs what took place in the past.

Strategies Against Satan

The Holy Spirit is empowering believers in numerous ways to counteract the advances of the devil. For example, the House of Prayer for All Nations, located on the Mount of Olives and directed by Tom Hess, is currently open 24 hours a day so people can intercede for the nations of the world. It is also a center for discipleship training.

Leaders in the believing communities in Jerusalem are moving beyond disagreements to a place of unity. Their ability to supersede theological differences provides a major testimony to the emerging unity among the Body of Christ. Praise God that healthier relationships have begun to form.

Younger leaders are moving into pastoral roles, as well as into many prophetic and apostolic ministries in Israel.

Believers are reaching out to secular Israel through music and television programs that feature testimonies from believers. A growing number of Israelis are accepting Jesus Christ through this media ministry. A deep hunger tugs at young people who have not found satisfaction in the materialism prevalent in their society. God is moving in magnificent ways to gather souls from His vineyard.

The spiritual temperature in Israel is rising due to the many conflicts surrounding its people. Believers realize they must have an intimate walk with the Lord to be effective. Many are recommitting themselves not only to reach the lost but also to live a sanctified life. Others who see this are drawn to the believers, opening doors of opportunity for the believers to testify to the love of the Savior.

When Jewish people become followers of the Way, they link with a part of the wider Body. The kingdom of God has seen a great influx of Jewish believers since the 1960s. It is clear that every day more Jews are embracing Jesus as their Savior. Intercessors should also invest more prayer effort to reach Jews in positions of power. As believers, their testimonies could reach a wide circle of people.

Leaders in the believing communities in Israel are encouraged by what God is doing among them. Their hearts are focused on sharing the Gospel with their people. Young people especially are being reached in increasing numbers, providing great hope for reconciliation. When the relationship between believers in Israel is free of animosity and distrust, there can be true fellowship, dialogue, and unity in Body of Christ. Jesus said that the world would know we are His disciples by our love—not by our denomination, church government, or distinctive doctrines, but by our love for one another (John 13:35).

Pray for the Peace of Jerusalem!

Jesus prayed for the city of Jerusalem during His earthly ministry (Luke 13:34-35). All believers should have the same affection for the "city of the great King." Many disparate voices would attempt to lead us to think or act a certain way regarding Jerusalem and its inhabitants. Before we eagerly trot off down some path, we must always remember to seek God concerning his heart for the city.

In Luke 13:34, Jesus wept over the city that killed the prophets and stoned the messengers God had sent. His tears for Jerusalem were tears of compassion. Can we today feel any less for this city that has seen such turmoil and ruin during its long history? Psalm 122:6 encourages us, "Pray for the peace of Jerusalem." As we are faithful to intercede, God will answer our prayers for this city that is dear to Him.

However, it is important to remember that God does not lay aside the attribute of justice to dispense mercy. An article entitled "Jerusalem as Jesus Views It" by Calvin E. Shenk in *Christianity Today* explains the challenges facing us:

"Some [believers], instead of calling Jerusalem to repentance, only bless Jerusalem and emphasize God's promises, ignoring the conditional nature of God's promises. Jerusalem is not exempt from God's will revealed in Jesus. Justice for all parties is more important than absolute sovereignty over Jerusalem...

"Jesus wept because Jerusalem did not understand the things that make for peace (Luke 19:42). Can the 'City of Peace' discover today the things that make for peace?...Will [the faith of believers] foster or hamper efforts for justice, peace, and security for all? [Believers] need to pray (Ps. 122:6), act, and hope for the peace of Jerusalem, a peace built upon the foundation of justice, a peace for all the people of Israel and Palestine.

"Jerusalem is one of the few places in the world considered holy to several religions....Justice and human rights call for a shared Jerusalem for [all inhabitants of the Land]...Jerusalem is not only important for the religion [of all parties], but each of these groups lives in Jerusalem. The claims of local people to Jerusalem should not be minimized. There will be no peace if some groups are excluded...

"In Jerusalem Jesus prayed that believers might be one (John 17:20-23). Churches need to transcend their particular histories, renounce prejudice, and work for mutual understanding. As a symbol, the...church of Jerusalem can help [believers] transcend their particular community affiliations. Today there are hopeful signs of increasing unity among

Jerusalem's churches, both among Palestinian [believers] and between Jewish believers in Jesus. [Believers] from abroad should help to heal division rather than increase fragmentation.

"Palestinian [believers] are a minority within a minority. The diminishing number of [Palestinian believers] in the region due to emigration is of great concern to the [believing] community. Archbishop of Canterbury George Carey, on a visit to Jerusalem in 1992, expressed hope that the diminishing number of [believers] would not result in an 'empty theme park.' How tragic if the church should cease to be meaningfully present in the city where it was born.

"How can [believers] be an authentic presence in Jerusalem? Surely the living [faith] community, (the temple of Jesus), is of greater significance than the Temple Mount. Community-centered faith is more important than site-centered faith."[13]

Pray that God would hasten the day among believers in His beloved Jerusalem when the walls that divide them would be obliterated. May there rise up among believers in the Holy Land a group of committed, dedicated servants who look beyond the things that keep them apart to the Holy One of Israel, who alone is the King of kings and Lord of lords.

You Can Help Meet the Challenge

- Pray that believers from other countries will be sensitive to the fact that there are Messianic Jews, Palestinian and Arab believers, and MBBs living in the land.
- When you tour Israel, worship with these believers and encourage them while you're there.
- Partner with Messianic, Palestinian and Arab believers, and Arab MBBs to meet special needs they may have in the land.
- Keep informed about the complex issues shaping the spiritual climate in Jerusalem and the Middle East.
- Pray for the peace of Jerusalem!

Endnotes

1. Source: *The Guardian*, 3 December, 1998 by David Sharrock

2. Source: Labib Madanat, December 18, 1998

3. Source: Labib Madanat, July 28, 1998

4. Source: Ray G. Register, Jr., *Back to Jerusalem, Church Planting in the Holy Land*, Baptist Village 45875, Israel, 1997, page 90 (unpublished manuscript)

5. Source: *Christianity Today*, April 7, 1997 pages 36,37, "Sharing living water: an innovative desert ministry breaks down walls between Arab and Jewish believers," by S. Aaron Osborne.

6. Source: Generals of Intercession's *G.I. News*, April–May 1996, pp. 4, 12; "Israel: A Nation Divided—The Church Striving for Unity" by Chuck D. Pierce; used by permission

7. Source: E-mail from Ray Register to Luis Bush, December 10, 1998

8. Ibid

9. Source: "Christians protest proposed 'anti-missionary' legislation," *Christianity Today*, May 19, 1997, page 55 by S. Aaron Osborne

10. Source: Interview with David Friedman at Christian Information Network, 11 June 1998

11. Fiqh (Jurisprudence and Islamic Rulings) Alhudood WatTa'azeerat (Punishment and Judicial Sentences) from www.islam-qa.com

12. Source: *Christianity Today*, 13 July 1998, p. 14

13. Calvin E. Shenk, "Jerusalem as Jesus Views It," *Christianity Today*, 5 October 1998 (Vol. 42, No. 11), pp. 44ff; used by permission

9

Paradigm Shifts in Global Missions

The 20th century has seen a surge of interest in religion. We are living in a time of unprecedented global revival. In a 1990 follow-up to the 1982 bestseller *Megatrends,* John Naisbitt and Patricia Aburdene write in *Megatrends 2000* about the tenth megatrend identified in the earlier book. The chapter "Religious Revival of the Third Millennium" describes the "unmistakable signs of a worldwide multi-denominational religious revival."[1]

The "God is dead" philosophy of the 1960s has been replaced. To quote *Megatrends 2000* again, "With the millennium in sight, the powerful countertrend of the religious revival is repudiating blind faith in science and technology."[2]

The focus of mission within Christendom has changed also. As Naisbitt and Aburdene write, "The year 2000 is operating like a powerful magnet on humanity, already reaching down into the 1990s and intensifying the decade. It is amplifying emotions, accelerating change, and heightening awareness, compelling us to re-examine ourselves, our values and our institutions."[3]

Examining Our Ministry Structures

Youth With A Mission (YWAM), one of the largest evangelical organizations in the world, exemplifies this new reality. In recent years, YWAM has restructured itself to focus on reaching the unreached people groups in the 10/40 Window. Beyond 2000, this trend undoubtedly will accelerate among other organizations.

In 1997 Paul Filidis, Office Director of YWAM International Communications Network, gave the following update on YWAM'S activities in the 10/40 Window: "We are indeed grateful for the growth of our mission in the so-called '10/40 Window' countries. Following the increased call to reach the unreached, we have seen a definite increase of staff residing within that part of the world. Over the past six years, the percentage of staff that lives in the 10/40 Window rose from nine percent in 1991, to 16 percent in 1997 (in actual numbers from 630 to 1651). We have established a presence in nine more countries within the Window totaling 41 nations."[4]

God is calling all of us to reexamine our structures. During my most recent trip to Norway, I (Luis) learned about the new vision of one of that nation's largest missions organizations. The Norwegian Santal Mission is under the leadership of Torbjorn Lied, who also chairs the Norwegian Missionary Council. Lied spoke of the complete renewal of his mission to focus on the unfinished task of world evangelism. Praise God!

Revitalization of Missions through the Church

George Verwer, who leads the AD2000 network for mobilization of new missionaries, received a vision concerning the mobilization of 200,000 new missionaries, primarily for the 10/40 Window. This concept is a breakthrough in missions strategy. It is based on the idea that each life-giving church should be responsible to affirm, support, and commission people from their own congregation to go to the mission field.[5]

God is calling the Church to revitalize missions. The early Church practiced sending members from their own congregations to preach the Gospel. The church in Antioch commissioned Paul and Barnabas. (Acts 11:22, 29; Acts 13:1-5.)

In the above biblical example, we can see an emerging pattern in the Church today. Instead of relying solely on "sending agencies" to place workers on the mission field, God is asking His people to reexamine how we can facilitate a greater number of individuals to fulfill their call as "missionaries." No organization is better equipped to determine who has a calling for missions than the local church.

Sending people from a local congregation into the harvest fields requires commitment by the local body of believers. First, there must be an ongoing commitment to prayer on the part of the senders for those who are being sent. Regular prayer will help keep those on the mission field from discouragement, ineffectiveness, and the attacks of the enemy. A commitment to cover missionaries in prayer will enable them to accomplish the task for which they have been sent. Without proper prayer coverage the likelihood of failure increases.

Next, the congregation and missionaries must invest time to build a strong support base. Paul and Barnabas spent considerable time with the believers in Antioch. Working, worshiping, praying, and learning together, the church knew the character and spiritual condition of these two men. They were faithful to the Lord and committed to His people, plans, and purposes.

Finally, there must be a commitment of finances. In order for Paul and Barnabas to devote their time and talents to the work of the Gospel, they were supported financially by fellow believers (2 Cor. 8:1-4; Phil. 4:15, 16).

Today, there are churches where members have a call on their lives for missions. However, smaller churches may not have the finances to support them while they are on the mission field. The Body of Christ has a responsibility to provide the necessary means for them to carry out their call to missions. Through financial and technical support, larger churches can assist smaller churches in sending others to evangelize the unreached.

Empowering the Next Generation

Another paradigm shift is the concerted effort to equip the next generation to carry on where we leave off. We have yet to tap into the resources of the next generation. There are Davids and Esthers strategically placed on the earth by God during this critical time in human history to be leaders in the effort to reach the lost and plant churches. They are visionaries and strategists who need to be equipped, encouraged, empowered, and made aware of the vast possibilities before them. We must do whatever it takes to release them into their destiny. The Church should focus on discipling, training, and mentoring them in order to improve their ability to serve effectively.

Among the resources available in Generation X are international students attending universities in the religiously free world. The Church must be alert and realize the contribution that these students can bring to the missions mandate. According to Tom Phillips, President of International Students Inc. in Colorado Springs, Colorado, 75 percent of these students, after acquiring a degree, will return to their country of origin. They will hold positions of importance and will influence the future of their countries. A large percentage of these students are from 10/40 Window countries where we cannot openly send missionaries, such as China, Iran, Iraq, Libya, and Saudi Arabia. God in His mercy is sending them to our doorsteps so that we can witness to them.

Now is the time to take up the challenge to tell international students about the love of the Savior. We must not let this opportunity slip from our grasp. If there is a college or university near you that has international students, seek out ministries already working on the campus to reach these students. Consider investing a few hours a week to share your faith with them. Reaching these students for Christ enhances the influence of the Gospel globally.

A New Breed for a New Millennium

Another significant trend in these latter days spotlights how the Holy Spirit is drawing a greater number of missionaries to the 10/40 Window who have an intimate relationship with Jesus Christ. Their strong commitment to the Lord creates in them the strong desire to serve and please Him.

Because of His infinite love, these missionaries know that their Father in heaven yearns to reach the lost. These believers have developed a longing in their hearts to see the Window nations come to the Lord and share in the eternal life offered by His beloved Son. Their compassion for the lost runs so deep that these believers are willing to live out the Scripture in Revelation 12:11: "They did not love their lives so much as to shrink from death." They are willing to endure hardships, go without creature comforts, and sacrifice their lives as an offering for the Lord to see the lost come to Him.

These missionaries may not do missions by the book. God gives them innovative ideas on how to reach the lost people groups who take a top priority on His agenda. He affirms them among the unreached peoples they serve, as He did with Old Testament leaders and the apostles. These saints are driven to do things for God's glory and not their own. They do things His way, not the way of the world. They are unique, anointed, and appointed by God for such a time as this.

As the Holy Spirit captures the hearts of more and more believers, they will burn with passion for Jesus, as well as have His zeal and compassion for the lost. Through their dedication to the Great Commission, the nations of the world will be transformed.

These present and future missionaries carry on the legacy of men and women who on the vast foreign mission fields of the world laid the foundation for our present endeavors with their dedication, commitment, vision, and sometimes the sacrifice of their lives. Because of their energy, love, and compassion for the unreached, we now are experiencing the fruit of their labors. We are continuing to build on the foundation that they faithfully laid. Methods that they employed to evangelize the lost were very effective, and many of their methods are still used today. Yet, God is opening new avenues and strategies for missions into the next century.

Flexible Leadership Style to Complete the Great Commission

Current trends in organizational development reflect styles that will prove most effective in the 21st century. A series of contrasts best illustrate these changes in organizational philosophy and procedures. The emerging leadership model emphasizes personal relationship over positional relationship. The style is less structured and more flexible. The focus of loyalty has shifted from institutions to people. The source of energy comes from change and innovation rather than stability. Instead of dogmatic and authoritative leadership, effective organizations now emphasize a leadership style that is inspirational, empowering, enabling, and facilitating. Rather than giving orders, the leader now coaches and teaches. Instead of a standard of quality dependent on the affordable best, the organization calls forth excellence. Associates' expectations center more on personal growth and less on security. Status comes not from title and rank but from making a difference. An effective organization considers its most valuable resources as not so much cash and time, but rather information, people, and networks. This is the wave of the future—beyond 2000.

We see the move of the Holy Spirit in powerful ways in the 10/40 Window as a major trend of our times. Simultaneously, however, we also observe the move of Satan to oppose the advance of God in the 10/40 Window. Thus, the Church worldwide is beginning to move into the 10/40 Window with prayer and people, in a concerted effort, cooperating together in renewed organizations with a more flexible style of leadership in order to complete the mandate of preaching the Gospel to the entire world.

Indigenous Missions

Another paradigm shift is the rise of indigenous missions. In many countries the activities of foreign missionaries have been hindered, in part, by a growing reluctance by certain governments to allow outside religious workers into their countries. Leaders of some countries are suspicious of missionaries' motives and therefore prohibit them from entering.

National Christian workers have advantages over foreign workers, and more and more nationals are taking up the challenge to reach their country's citizens with the Gospel. They already know the language and customs of the people they are trying to reach. They understand the culture and the mindset of those with whom they are working.

Foreign missionaries must learn the culture, language, and customs—and spend great amounts of money and time to do so. Often missions-sending agencies require theological degrees and training, which also involve time and money. While there is a great need for both foreign and indigenous missionaries, in many cases it is more cost effective to support nationals in ministry within their own country.

Unity and Strategic Alliances

In order for the Body of Christ to overcome spiritual darkness, believers must repent of ways we have cooperated with the enemy. Many of the Window churches suffer from lack of unity and cooperation. James 4:1-3 warns against such quarrels. We have heard horror stories about pastors turning in other church leaders to governmental officials because someone else's church was flourishing more than their own. This has happened in Window churches more often than we would like to admit. Much prayer is required to ensure that jealousy, envy, and disunity do not prevail among the believers and ministries in the 10/40 Window. It would serve the cause of the Gospel and the Great Commission if we would remember the words of the apostle Paul in Ephesians 4:3-6: "Make every effort to keep the unity of the Spirit through the bond of peace. There is one body, and one Spirit—just as you were called to one hope when you were called—one Lord, one faith, one baptism; one God and Father of all, who is over all and through all and in all."

What can be done to break the powers of darkness that have penetrated the Church? Jesus' high priestly prayer for all believers in John 17:20-26 gives insight into overcoming the plans Satan has unleashed against the Church. We should pray according to Jesus' petition in John 17:24 that the Body of Christ be brought to complete unity as a witness that He is the Son of the Living God. Following Christ's model of servanthood and humility found in Philippians 2:5-9 is an effective means to demolish the powers of darkness.

As the Church learns to network and build strategic alliances and partnerships, we have discovered a key principle. Working together in concert is much more effective than each ministry trying to work alone. A story is told about two prized draft horses that finished first and second at a county fair competition. The grand champion horse pulled a sled with 4,500 pounds on it; the runner-up pulled 4,400 pounds. Someone wondered how many pounds the two horses could pull together. It would be reasonable to assume that the horses would double their capacity. But that was not the case. Hitched together as a team, they were able to pull more than 12,000 pounds![6]

The global Church can learn from this example, which is the same principle as presented in Leviticus 26:8: "Five of you will chase a hundred, and a hundred of you will chase ten thousand, and your enemies will fall by the sword before you." In Psalm 133, the Lord commands a blessing when we come together in unity. Churches and ministries that have similar visions and focuses are forming strategic alliances to complete a particular task. Some of these alliances aim for technological advancement, while other alliances are field-based, consisting of nationals and bi-vocational workers actively endeavoring in concert to advance the Kingdom of God. Other networks have a common focus on a particular unreached people. Still other associations are resource-based, seeking to generate and supply greater resources to complete the unfinished task of taking the Gospel to the ends of the earth.

The AD2000 and Beyond Movement is one notable example of an effective strategic alliance working within the 10/40 Window and worldwide. The network has more than 1,000 Christian organizations, churches, and ministries focusing on the unique cultural and religious issues of each region. The AD2000 United Prayer Track, linking prayer movements throughout the globe, in turn gave birth to the *Praying Through*

The Window initiatives that have mobilized united prayer across churches, countries, and continents.

Each of the *Praying Through The Window* coordinating committees has brought together key leaders from various ministries. Dick Eastman, International President of Every Home, chaired the first prayer initiative. Michael Little, President and Chief Operating Officer of Christian Broadcasting Network chaired *Praying Through The Window II, III* and *IV.* Senior pastor of New Life Church in Colorado Springs, Ted Haggard is the co-founder of the World Prayer Center and founder of the Christian Information Network (CIN). CIN serves as the administrative arm for the *Praying Through The Window* committees. The committe provides the funding for the ministry of *Praying Through The Window,* while New Life Church provides the office space, equipment, and personnel for CIN to serve as a nerve center for the global 10/40 Window prayer movement.

The World Prayer Center in Colorado Springs is another example of strategic partnership among organizations with complementary goals. Beginning with a vision God gave Pastor Haggard, he and New Life Church committed to establishing a prayer center that would coordinate intercession for global evangelization across the entire Body of Christ. Dedicated in September 1998, the World Prayer Center now houses the Christian Information Network, Global Harvest Ministries, the Wagner Institute for Practical Ministry, and the Arsenal Bookstore and Resource Center. In addition, George Otis Jr., founder and President of the Sentinel Group in Seattle, Washington, co-labors with the World Prayer Center staff to provide strategic information from around the world. C. Peter Wagner, president of the World Prayer Center, anticipates linking with local prayer rooms in 5,000 U.S. churches and national prayer networks in 120 other countries by the year 2000.

Victories and Counterattacks

As the church reclaims more and more ground for the kingdom of God, the enemy will continue to strike back. We will see this trend happen throughout the 10/40 Window in a stronger degree than ever before because Satan knows his end is near. Christian Information Network received an insightful e-mail from Joseph Ozawa, describing current trends in the 10/40 Window. Ozawa holds a doctorate in psychology and is Senior Psychologist for the Ministry of Community Development in Singapore. He is also a core faculty member of Bethany School of Missions and a licensed Anglican minister.

There is widespread interest, Ozawa noted, in strategic intercession prayerwalking, prayer mapping, and other such developments in prayer among God's people around the world. Fervor runs high for intercession. Meetings in some countries have been dramatic and incredibly powerful, notably in Singapore, the Philippines, Malaysia, Kenya, India, and Hong Kong. Miracles in answer to prayer occur frequently. One recent example was the closure and "wipe out" of the Temple of 10,000 Buddhas in Hong Kong, one of the most significant strongholds of the enemy in the 10/40 Window area. This took place while the body of Christ was praying for Hong Kong during the return of the territory to Communist China.

On 1 July 1997 the Buddhists were poised for a massive takeover as well. Their points of power included the Temple of 10,000 Buddhas in Shatin, construction one of the largest outdoor Buddha statues in the world on Lantau Island, the bringing of a gigantic incense bowl to Hong Kong, and a dramatic and spectacular rally of Buddhists from all over Asia at an outdoor stadium in Hong Kong.

Hong Kong Christians, who for many months had interceded and repented of idolatry, began a spiritual offensive. Many were even led to pray for "big monsoon rains" to stop the Buddhist festivities. In the days following the takeover, the biggest recorded rainfall in Hong Kong's history hit the city! The rain greatly dampened the Buddhists' outdoor activities. To the delight of Hong Kong intercessors, a landslide hit the Temple of 10,000 Buddhas, causing walls to collapse and idols to fall into the mud. Then, for safety reasons, the government ordered the temple shut. The center of Buddhist idolatry on the road from Hong Kong to mainland China was closed for good! The Asian church was fired up by this victory and continues to this day to pray with increased fervor.

The intense spiritual battle rages on. Now is no time for complacency or triumphalism. The enemy strikes back after waiting for us to let our guard down. Many nations face a strong resurgence of militant Islam, Hinduism, Buddhism, and various cults, with attempts to suppress and even destroy all vestiges of Christianity.

Worldwide, Satan is working to render the Church ineffective. Dissension between evangelical, charismatic, and Pentecostal groups is ripping apart the church in many nations, especially in Japan. At the same time, Orthodox and Catholic churches seem intent on battling evangelicals as they gain prominence in many countries, including Ethiopia. Satan is also using materialism (mammon) to lull the Church to sleep. In many countries, such as the United States, South Korea, and Singapore, the churches are big and comfortable. Millions are spent on buildings. Some churches in these countries expend considerable energy, time, and resources competing with one another. The enemy also attacks churches through syncretism, especially in the 10/40 Window. In Africa, for instance, witchcraft is mixed with Christianity. In some Eastern nations, animism is combined with Christianity. Another damaging influence has come through the resurgence of worldly attitudes and lifestyles filtering into the Church. We are losing a sense of holiness or separation from the practices and thinking of the unsaved people around us. The Church is ceasing to be distinct from the world.

There has been—and will undoubtedly be—an ongoing battle with strident Islam. Militant Hinduism in India is on the rise. Buddhists and Hindus are learning to do spiritual mapping, prayerwalking, and strategic intercession! (In one church building, Buddhists monks were actually found praying against the Christian believers.)

God Raising Leaders from Two-thirds World Countries

One of the most exciting trends of the past several years has come out of Latin America. Unprecedented numbers of cross-cultural missionaries are arising from Latin American countries, and many have headed to the 10/40 Window. The Holy Spirit has prepared the way by giving common cultural values that win these Latins increased receptivity among the people groups they want to reach.

Latin American leaders from Youth With A Mission, for example, met at a 1997 Prayer Summit in Sumatra, Indonesia, and reported their observations with respect to the local Chantik people group. "As Latins we discovered so many similarities between the Chantik and Latin cultures, e.g., the desire to make friends from the beginning, a similar lifestyle, [and] how we perceive the culture that surrounds us. All this even though we are separated by thousands of miles and speak a different language. We believe these similarities have been prepared by God to enable Latins easy access to work among the Chantik and in Indonesia as a whole."

Explosion of Radio and Television Evangelism

In the United States, an elderly woman confined to a wheelchair attends church by watching a television broadcast presented by her local church. Chinese believers huddle around a small radio set attending "church" by listening to a Christian broadcast. In an Indian village, several of the local congregations gather around a television set, watching a discipleship course being beamed across Asia via satellite. In the Middle East, hundreds of thousands of Kurds turn on their own televisions and pick up evangelistic programming via satellite.

The impact of radio and television broadcasting is the equivalent of a spiritual shock wave throughout the world. These media have been able to reach those who can't go to church, those who don't have a church, and those who don't have any concept of the Gospel.

Evangelistic coverage to non-regular listeners is far more extensive; currently, 4.6 billion people can receive Christian broadcasting in their mother tongue.

Available information indicates that 900 million Christians regularly listen to Christian radio and television. Of these, 51 million are bedridden listeners and 20 million are "radio/television believers"—that is, they have no local church and depend on the broadcasts for discipleship, training, and fellowship.[7]

I (Luis) expounded on this trend in a 1998 report: "In the Arabian Peninsula, Saudi citizens have invested billions of dollars in the development of international satellite television. By the end of 1997, 70 percent of all homes had a satellite dish. An estimated 90,000 new homes receive their first satellite dish each month. Officially, satellite dishes are illegal in Saudi Arabia! However, the growth of satellite television in this 'closed' Islamic nation has made it possible for the Gospel to penetrate the Arab world. SAT7, an evangelical cooperative satellite initiative, began broadcasting two hours of Christian programming per week in 1997. In 1998, the total increased to nine hours of programming weekly."[8] Other satellite companies have also been beaming programming into Arab countries, including Middle East Television.

The results are astounding. Because of Christian broadcasting, the Church averages 3 million new believers per year in a total of 200 countries. Of these, 400,000 are isolated radio converts. Ten thousand new isolated house churches spring into existence every year as a consequence of radio and television programs.

What happens to these believers? Many access correspondence courses from the broadcasters, which they can use to further their own discipleship. Some receive direct training via the broadcasts, learning how to share the Gospel and evangelize their neighbors. Radio programs greatly aid the spread of Christianity in restricted access countries. Eventually, "radio churches" spring up—congregations of believers that meet and listen to radio broadcasts for their worship services. These churches often contact believers in other parts of the world to receive support, then evangelize their neighbors. A cell of ten Christians today could become a major church of 1,000 believers next year.

There is still a greater need for broadcast evangelism. In many languages, Christian broadcasting totals a scant 15 or 30 minutes per week. The airtime allotted for broadcasts in many language groups is not nearly enough for groups whose language may be spoken by millions.[9] We believe more and more ministries will be responding to this need in the next few years.

Illiteracy: Blindness to the Word of God

Another trend is highlighted by Justin Long, managing editor of the "Monday Morning Reality Check," a weekly editorial distributed via the Internet through Global Evangelization Movement and World Evangelization Research Center. Following is a summary of his conclusions:

One of the most powerful tools for evangelization, of course, is the Bible. A portion of the Bible or its entirety has been translated into more than 2,000 languages. It is estimated that 1.4 billion copies of Scriptures portions, New Testaments, or the whole Bible are distributed every year. The impact is enormous. The Bible League states that on average, for every Bible distributed in China, five converts are the direct result. Certainly, evangelization efforts among any people group are severely hampered by the absence of Scripture, and the lack of Bibles among Christians yields the potential for error and heresy.

However, even when the Scriptures are translated into the language of unreached people groups, a substantial barrier remains that many Christians interested in world evangelization haven't considered. This is the widespread problem of illiteracy. Nearly one in five people on our planet cannot read. Film and broadcast media are an excellent way to reach those who cannot read. This is why Campus Crusade for Christ's *JESUS* film has been so effective.

Illiteracy affects not only Bible distribution but also other media outreach efforts. Simply translating and distributing the Scriptures, in many cases, will not be enough. We must teach people to read the Scriptures as well. Governments hostile to Christianity will sometimes welcome educational programs, including literacy programs. Charitable givers should find out if there is a literacy program attached to a Bible translation project and determine its level of funding in comparison to the project as a whole. Literacy programs may deserve special funding.[10]

Meanwhile, until more people are taught to read, using innovative and creative ways to present the Gospel in interesting and compelling formats can substantially circumvent the barriers of illiteracy. Dramas depicting various stories from the Bible can be developed in the primary language of the people who need to be reached. Worship that is presented in a culturally sensitive manner, using instruments, dance, or other idioms familiar to the people in a region, is another excellent means to reach those who are illiterate. Door-to-door evangelism, with its personal approach, can prove effective in sharing one's faith. Preaching by nationals or visiting ministers, accompanied by a translator if necessary, can be used by God to bring illiterate people to Jesus.

Martyrdom Is the Natural State of the Church

Martyrdom has increased dramatically in this century and even qualifies as a paradigm shift in our thinking. Since the very beginning of Christianity, there has never been a century free of persecution or martyrdom. Though we are horrified at accounts of imprisonment, torture, enslavement, humiliation, rape, and martyrdom, it must be remembered that persecution and martyrdom is the normal state of the church.

As plans for global evangelization continue into the next millennium, extremists and repressive governments will continue to oppose the Gospel. Opposition will continue to be hostile. Efforts to reach the unevangelized currently employ one percent of the available mission force. In 1997, 160 thousand believers were martyred for their faith. If the number of missionaries involved in the effort to reach the unevangelized grows from one percent to five percent, we may see the number of martyrs increase to five times the number cited above. Here are three hypothetical scenarios of how the next century's martyr situation might appear:

Scenario 1: 10/40 Window plans falter out of fear.

The publicity and cost of the first martyrs leads to fear and a dampening of interest in missions to the 10/40 Window. Plans for global evangelism falter, and the number of martyrs declines as Christians retreat.

Scenario 2: Hard effort.

Growing energy is devoted to plans for global evangelization, spearheaded by Third-world nationals. Western governments refuse to intervene in what they term "religious issues" and warn mission agencies that they proceed at their own risk. Hundreds of thousands of new missionaries surge into restricted-access areas; the number of martyrs rises dramatically, reaching 400,000 per year by 2010, and 600,000 per year by 2025. By 2050 it tapers off to 250,000 annually as global evangelization draws to a close. Countries with an increased Christian presence soften persecution.

Scenario 3: The sacrifice of the next generation.

With the advent of AD2000, a new, determined, sustained push for world evangelization begins as Third-world indigenous personnel and Western youth take up the banner. Satellites, Internet communications, itinerant tourists, widespread signs and wonders, and a veritable invasion of young people take the world unaware. The number of martyrs increases to 1 million by 2010. The sight of young people executed causes world condemnation, global evangelization is a reality by 2012, and massive church growth occurs over the next ten years as martyrdom decreases to 300,000 per year.

These are hypothetical scenarios and statistics, of course, but every agency and individual believer needs to consider these issues, devote themselves to prayer, and reexamine their own level of commitment. Missionaries should have contingency plans covering the possibility of arrest, imprisonment, suffering, and martyrdom. After all, this was the attitude and expectation of the Early Church, and it mirrored the command of Christ to "take up your cross and follow Me." When we take up that cross, we ought to be in possession of a total commitment to the end.[11]

Window Opportunities: The Next Steps and a Vision

What are the next steps for God's kingdom in the 10/40 Window? In the search for a trend, both Scripture and current world reports suggest that the situation is going to get worse, not better. Revelation 12:7-9 describes a future scene: "And there was war in heaven. Michael and his angels fought against the dragon, and the dragon and his angels fought back. But he was not strong enough, and they lost their place in heaven. The great dragon was hurled down—that ancient serpent called the devil, or Satan, who leads the whole world astray. He was hurled to the earth, and his angels with him." Verse 12 reads, "He is filled with fury, because he knows that his time is short." The devil will suffer final defeat, but his wrath will cause the earth and its inhabitants much suffering before then.

Knowing this truth will help us prepare for the future. Let us follow the Apostle Paul's counsel in Ephesians 4:12-16 "to prepare God's people for works of service, so that the body of Christ may be built up until we all reach unity in the faith…and become mature, attaining to the whole measure of the fullness of Christ… Instead, speaking the truth in love, we will in all things grow up into him who is the Head, that is, Christ. From him the whole body, joined and held together by every supporting ligament, grows and builds itself up in love, as each part does its work."

At the same time, we can take hope, knowing that God's kingdom will continue to advance until the earth is filled with the knowledge of the glory of the Lord. The progress mirrors a vision given to Tommi Femrite, an intercessor, on 28 September 1997:

"During worship I had a vision of the 10/40 Window with layers of curtains over it. The first curtain was a 'blackout shade' like the kind used during the war. It totally blacked out all light. I saw that this curtain has been removed—lifted. The second curtain was 'opaque.' Only the indication of light could be detected, but one could not see people, places, or faces. This, too, has been removed—lifted. The third curtain was 'translucent.'

Light now shines through. We can see movement and forms but we cannot make out faces or details.

"Then I saw people from around the world holding cords attached to this curtain. The Lord is ready to give His command to lift this curtain, to remove the canopy, to lift the veil. And as we pull together through prayer, His light and His glory will shine clearly through the Window to illuminate the people for us.

"In thinking about these curtains, I believe they have been removed through *Praying Through The Window I, II, and III.* I believe there is a fourth curtain. It is transparent. Light flows through it unimpeded so that we now see the people, places, and faces distinctly. This curtain must also be lifted. It stands between the Lord and the people of the 10/40 Window— between the Lord and the part of His Bride who yet lives in darkness. We must join together, pulling the cords to this curtain through prayer to let Jesus, the Light of the world, shine brightly on each face. My expectations run high for *Praying Through The Window IV.* May the Lord's glory and presence shine brightly on the peoples and nations of the 10/40 Window."[12]

You Can Help Meet the Challenge

- Take advantage of the current resurgence of interest in religion and spirituality to share the Good News of Jesus Christ with seekers.
- Pray that God will use current events and societal shifts to open the door for greater receptivity to the Gospel.
- Evaluate your ministry styles and patterns and be willing to change models and network with others for greater effectiveness.
- Intercede for the Lord to break the strongholds of disunity, materialism, syncretism, and worldliness in the Church.
- Seek deeper devotion and commitment to the Lord and His purposes, so He can use you as a radical world-changer.
- Christian radio or television broadcasters can increase programming directed toward the unevangelized world.

- Christian donors can allocate a portion of their giving toward broadcast projects specifically in the 10/40 Window.
- Foreign mission boards and agencies can seek ways to follow up on write-in responses to their broadcasts.
- Broadcasters can take on new 10/40 Window languages in their viewership.
- Christian foundations can fund projects involving translating evangelistic and discipleship series into 10/40 Window languages for large-scale broadcast.[13]

Endnotes

1. Quoted by Jay Rogers in his review, "Megatrends authors predict spiritual awakening for the 1990s," in *The Forerunner,* September 1990. Reprinted by permission from Media House International, Melbourne, Florida
2. Ibid.
3. John Naisbitt and Patricia Aburdene, *Megatrends 2000* (William Morrow, 1990)
4. 1997 YWAM International Survey by Paul Filidis, Director of Youth With A Mission's International Communications office based in Colorado Springs, CO USA
5. George Verwer, International founder and Director of Operation Mobilization
6. Source: John C. Maxwell, *Developing the Leaders Around You,* Nashville: Thomas Nelson, 1995, pp. 11–12
7. Justin Long, "Megatrend #6: The Mushrooming of Radio/TV Christianity," Monday Morning Reality Check #38, 1996
8. "Global Trends & Mission, with a Special Focus on the 10/40 Window," by Luis Bush, report for a spring 1998 conference in Cyprus
9. Justin Long, "Megatrend 6: Mushrooming of radio/TV Christianity" Monday Morning Reality Check # 38, 1996
10. Justin Long, "Illiteracy: Blindness to the Word of God," Monday Morning Reality Check #23, 1996
11. Justin Long, "The Future of Martyrdom," Monday Morning Reality Check #30, 1996
12. Source: Tommie Femrite; Intercessors International church in Bulverde, TX, 28 September 1997
13. Justin Long, "Megatrend #6: The Mushrooming of Radio/TV Christianity," Monday Morning Reality Check #38, 1996

10

Resources to Reach the Window

At a University of Texas Medical Branch clinic, I (Beverly) was drawn to a wall where the UTMB's Mission Statement declared, "The mission of the UTMB is to provide scholarly teaching, innovative scientific investigation, and state of the art patient care. UTMB must lead in the discovery of new approaches to the prevention and treatment of disease and in the application of this new knowledge. This effort requires superior patient care programs in each of its clinical departments which will, in turn, nurture and support scholarly activities that underlie and nurture them."

As I read this, I thought, "This is the type of heart the Body of Christ should have. We must be devoted to our compassionate desire to reach the lost." If a secular institution has this much dedication to healing people of disease, how much more should the Church provide for those who are diagnosed as eternally terminal—unless we reach them.

We must be willing to make cutting-edge changes in our approach in order to present the Gospel in a relational and culturally sensitive way in the darkest areas of the world. Since we have the mind of Christ (1 Cor. 2:16) and we have the Holy Spirit who searches out the things of God (1 Cor. 2:10) indwelling us (1 Cor. 3:16), we as God's people have access to heaven and all of its divine resources. Therefore, we must seek God for a release of His divine plan and purpose for the entire world (Isa. 14:24, 26).

Many people in the past have regarded the 10/40 Window nations and the people there as resistant to the Gospel. However, mission research expert David Barrett, editor of *World Christian Encyclopedia,* has concluded that the 10/40 Window is spiritually responsive to the Gospel. Christianity's poor representation in the 10/40 Window, he says, stems not from the people's resistance but simply from their lack of exposure to the Good News.[1]

"Dollar for dollar and hour for hour, the harvest coming from the 10/40 Window nations outstrips that from the rest of the world 100 to 1," Barrett says. "That is, if the same money and time spent to win one person to the Lord in the West were put to use in the 10/40 Window nations, the effort would yield a harvest of 100 souls added to the kingdom of God. It is 100 times more cost effective, therefore, to reach those in the 10/40 Window."[2]

The Church worldwide will have to give an account to the Lord for the way we spend our resources, continuing to retell the told when there are 1.4 billion people in the 10/40 Window who have never heard the glorious Gospel one time in a culturally sensitive way, in their own language. Author Oswald J. Smith, former pastor of Peoples Church in Toronto, Canada, has said, "No one deserves to hear the Gospel twice while there are those who have yet to hear it once."

This is the probing question we must ask ourselves: "Have we allocated people, resources, and finances properly, or have we squandered the gifts God has given us for reaching the lost on ourselves and our own pleasure?"

The Need for Skilled Bi-Vocational Workers

Directing our resources properly is all the more important in an age when completion of the Great Commission appears to be an attainable goal. As we face the 21st century, humankind boasts of greater technological advancement than at any other time in history. More knowledge than ever before is more readily available, especially on the Internet. Convenient transportation options abound. The Church enjoys enough wealth and finances to provide what is needed to bring the Good News to the 10/40 Window. Christianity claims more followers than any other religion, including Islam. We have the work force needed to finish the task.

Reaching the unreached of the 10/40 Window is possible. Secular business has proven this. Numerous businesses and franchises now stake a claim in the remotest parts of the world—Safeway, Chrysler Corporation, Kentucky Fried Chicken (KFC), McDonald's, Burger King, Pizza Hut, and others. Coca-Cola, for example, is available in 200 countries. The business world has already taken its products into places that the Church has yet to penetrate with the Gospel.

These same businesses can serve as ministry vehicles for the Body of Christ. Believers with skills sought after by the business world can provide an important resource to the kingdom of God. Those who travel and live cross-culturally under the auspices of their regular job find an entrée for the Gospel into otherwise resistant cultures and countries.

A recent conference I (Beverly) attended in Cyprus in the spring of 1998 included extensive discussion of "bi-vocational workers," also known as "tentmakers." One concern expressed was that when missionaries go on the field as tentmakers, their job-skill level might not attain a high enough standard. Excellence in the workplace wins favor and opens an avenue to share the Good News with co-workers. In other words, tentmakers may have strong spiritual skills, but weak job skills. If they have not made the necessary sacrifice to pursue excellence in their trade and gain the respect of their co-workers, tentmakers will be hindered in their witness to their colleagues, and perhaps even cast a bad light on other believers.

A different concern arises when bi-vocational workers who are high performers on the job isolate themselves from other believers in their country of ministry. Many do not associate with the local Body of Christ. When they forsake assembling together with other believers (Heb. 10:25, KJV), they become weak in their walk with the Lord.

Discipleship of Bi-Vocational Workers

As a Church we need to disciple younger people, just as Jesus discipled the Twelve, Moses discipled Joshua, and Paul discipled Timothy. The next generation presents a vast untapped bounty of skills and resources for the kingdom of God, both for bi-vocational work and full-time ministry. We must be dedicated to the discipleship of potential bi-vocational workers, encouraging them to pursue a deep relationship with the Lord. As we nurture them in their love for God and intimacy with Him, we can also pray for them as for our own children, desiring God's best for their lives. We can pray they would be compelled by the love of God to take the Good News to the spiritually dark places in the 10/40 Window. We need to instill in these bi-vocational workers (our spiritual children) a sense of the value of every human being created in the image of the invisible God. They can be reminded that it is an honor, as they obediently follow God's direction for their lives, to use the knowledge and skills they have obtained from colleges and universities and on-the-job training among people who don't know the love of Jesus Christ.

God calls us to be willing to send our best and most brilliant men and women, both those highly skilled in business or other vocations and those gifted in the five-fold ministry. It is our responsibility to pray for these workers to retain the mind and heart of Christ as they labor among the lost. No matter how ungodly the people they serve may appear to be, each of us must remember that these people are precious to the Lord and deserve our love and compassion. The lost are not simply faceless people to be added to our spiritual "hit lists." Each group has unique value to God. They deserve to know that our caring heavenly Father loved the world so much that He sent His only Son to rescue every single person on this planet from the ruthless grip of the devil.

A Tithing Church

Few of the Church's resources tend to provoke as much controversy as its finances. A sometimes not-so-silent majority feels uncomfortable whenever the Church begins to teach and speak about tithing. The Word of God is clear, as it declares in Malachi 3:10, that we are to tithe ten percent of the 100 percent of the first fruits (Prov. 3:9) that God gives us, and that the tithe is to go into the storehouse for the work of the Lord.

Over the past decade, the assets of the Church have grown enormously. Could it be that we have seen a tremendous growth in the wealth of the Church to prepare it for meeting its responsibility to fulfill the Great Commission? Increased income should be channeled to reach a ripe and burgeoning harvest field. The concept of the "graduated tithe" recognizes that as our income rises, we have proportionately fewer real needs of our own. Thus we can and should give a greater percentage of our income to God's work.

Annual giving to churches is tracked by *Giving USA,* a publication of the American Association of Fund-Raising Counsel/ Trust for Philanthropy.[3] In 1992 annual giving to North American churches or church-related activities totaled $56.7 billion. Latest figures for giving in 1997 total an estimated $66.26 billion.[4]

Statistics show an increase in the *amount* of giving; however, the *percentage* of income given by the majority of Christians has decreased. According to Ronald J. Sider, the percentage of income given has dropped from 3.14 percent in 1968 to 2.46 percent in 1995.[5] The New Testament is clear that giving to the Lord's work should not be *coerced*; however, we are *compelled* to give out of *love for the Savior.*

Paul deals with the subject of giving in many of his epistles. In 2 Corinthians he says that giving should not be done grudgingly. Our giving should be done out of gratitude for what Christ has done for us: "For you know the grace of our Lord Jesus Christ, that though he was rich, yet for your sakes he became poor, so that you through his poverty might be made rich" (2 Cor. 8:9).

How we spend our God-given resources is of paramount importance. We will all appear before the Lord one day to give an account of what we did while we were on earth. While Christians in the West live in relative luxury, the majority of the world's population ekes out a living on less than US $1.00 per day.[6] Can we honestly say that we are being good stewards of the riches God has given us? Each person must take an inventory of our expenditures. Billions of people are perishing without the knowledge of Jesus Christ. A reallocation of our income can mean the difference between souls spending eternity apart from God, or spending it in His presence.

Is the North American Church using its resources in the best way possible? Our mandate to complete the Great Commission should compel us to implement strategic plans for using the riches that God has entrusted to us to reach the lost worldwide. The billions who have yet to hear the Good News ought to have first claim on the billions of dollars Christians give yearly.

You Can Help Meet the Challenge

- Examine your resources—finances, time, skills—to see if they can be used more strategically to reach 10/40 Window peoples who have never heard the Gospel of Christ.
- Consider working as a tentmaker in areas closed to traditional evangelism. Disciple and encourage others toward bi-vocational ministry.
- Take a prayer journey to intercede on site for unreached people groups.
- Seek God's heart for the lost and perishing. Ask Him to motivate you with His love and compassion to do your part to fulfill the Great Commission.
- Explore creative options for ministry in difficult situations. Let God expand your faith that He can reach even the most closed and hidden peoples.
- If you are a Christian entrepreneur, investigate business opportunities in Window countries. This will give you an

opportunity to hire nationals and model the life of Christ in your business.

• Continue to intercede daily for the move of the Holy Spirit in the peoples and countries of the 10/40 Window.

Endnotes

1. David Barrett, phone interview with Luis Bush, 23 December 1997

2. David Barrett, phone interview with Luis Bush, 23 December 1997

3. John and Sylvia Ronsvalle, *The Christian Century,* 3 June 1998, p. 579

4. John and Sylvia Ronsvalle, *The Christian Century,* 3 June 1998, p. 58

5. Ronald J. Sider, President of Evangelicals for Social Action, *Charisma Magazine,* December 1998, p. 5

6. Ibid

EPILOGUE

Will the Church Respond to the Macedonia Call?

"The conclusion, when all has been heard, is: fear God and keep His commandments, because this applies to every person. For God will bring every act to judgment, everything which is hidden, whether it is good or evil" (Eccles. 12:13, 14 NAS).

Could these verses also apply to the Church using its finances, resources, and work force on those who have heard the Gospel message many times over?

This passage of Scripture applies to "every person"—including those in the Window. Yet they don't know the love of our God. They don't know they are supposed to worship God and not demonic deities. They don't know they should fear God. They haven't been taught His commandments. Why? They don't know, because the Church has neglected its responsibility to evangelize the Window countries.

This book is a clarion call to action. If we continue to ignore the spiritual cries of the people in the Window, we will have to answer to God.

"For some ethnolinguistic unreached people groups, it is 1,000 times more cost effective to spend our missions' resources on the lost in the 10/40 Window rather than on already evangelized Western countries," reports research expert David Barrett, editor of *World Christian Encyclopedia.* "It is outrageous for Christians to squander their limited evangelistic resources in heavily Christianized countries instead of the area where never-reached persons would hear the Good News for the first time.

"If we are to be good stewards of God's resources, doesn't it make sense to invest where the harvest is most plentiful? That is where we will see the greatest return for His kingdom."

These statements should resonate like God thundering from heaven, saying, "Wake up, Church, and direct your attention to the 10/40 Window. Now!"

In Matthew 24:14 it is clear that the Gospel must be preached in every nation before the end will come. The Gospel has not been preached to any measurable degree in the 10/40 Window. It is sobering to think that our disobedience could delay the Second Coming of Jesus Christ.

James 4:17 explains it this way: "Anyone, then, who knows the good he ought to do and doesn't do it, sins." After reading this book, we can no longer enter a plea of ignorance or naiveté.

We must channel laborers, finances, and resources immediately to the most spiritually needy area of the world—the 10/40 Window countries.

We cannot stop praying and seeking God for the release of His sovereign plan for the Window. When His strategies are released, we must be obedient and respond quickly to saturate the Window with the glorious Gospel of Jesus Christ. If we don't, we will be judged according to Ecclesiastes 12:13-14 for our disobedience and misappropriation of God's finances and resources.

You will find practical ways to do your part under "You Can Help Meet the Challenge" at the end of each chapter. Let's partner and join forces wherever we can to evangelize the Window. God may be calling you to labor hand-in-hand with ministries or people you never felt "called to" before. But if fulfilling the Great Commission is a "God idea"—one that comes from Him, not from us—we don't have to worry about who gets credit for completing the task. We simply have to lay aside our self-interests, pride, and competition in order to get the work done. That way, He gets all the honor and glory—not us.

Because of His zeal for the lost dwelling in the Window countries, there is no question that the Holy Spirit will make Jesus Christ known. The question is, "Will the Church move in concert with Him and be yielded vessels that He will use?" God *does* have a plan to reach the Window and He *will* accomplish this task by many or by few. Let's pray, fast, and seek God for the part each Christian is to play. Yes, each one of us is responsible to reach the lost in our generation.

The wind of the Holy Spirit is moving in the Window in an unprecedented way. The Lord desperately loves these precious lost ones. Let us join with the Holy Spirit of God to move methodically, effectively, and powerfully in the Window to introduce its inhabitants to Jesus Christ!

"From everyone who has been given much, much will be demanded; and from the one who has been entrusted with much, much more will be asked" (Luke 12:48).

Faces of the 10/40 Window

Photo courtesy of John Fries

Photo courtesy of John Fries

Photo courtesy of Ted Mehl

Photo courtesy of JESUS film project

Photo courtesy of JESUS film project

Photo courtesy of John Fries

Photo courtesy of John Fries

Photo courtesy of John Fries

Glossary

10/40 Window: The rectangular area of North Africa, the Middle East, and Asia between 10 and 40 degrees north latitude where 95 percent of the world's least evangelized people are found.

Animism: worship of nature and inanimate objects, such as rocks, trees, or clouds with the belief that spirits inhabit these objects.

Arab believer: one who lives in or comes from one of the countries of the Middle East and has placed his or her faith in Jesus Christ as Lord and Savior.

Arab Muslim Background Believer: one who lives in or comes from the Middle East who was a follower of Islam and has placed his or her faith in Jesus Christ as Lord and Savior.

Believer: one who has placed his or her faith in Jesus Christ as Lord and Savior.

Brahman caste: name of the highest class within Hinduism; to orthodox Hindus the people of this class are sacred.

Country: A nation or state, the territory of a nation or state, or the people of a nation or state.

Culturally sensitive: being able to present the Gospel to people in their own language through the Bible, film, etc. and present it in a cultural context which they can understand through music, stories, and instruments that are unique to that culture.

Ethnolinguistic: an ethnic or racial group speaking its own language. A people group distinguished by its self-identity with traditions of common descent, history, customs, and language.

Five religious blocs: the five blocs include Islam, Hinduism, Buddhism, Animism, and indigenous religions; all five blocs are headquartered in the 10/40 Window.

Gateway Cities: cities where decisions are made that will influence the spiritual, social, and economic status of a country.

Hajj: annual pilgrimage to Mecca, which all devout Muslims are obligated to make at least once in their lifetime.

Imam: a Muslim who serves as a spiritual leader of a mosque.

Indigenous missionary: a person working in or sent from his/her homeland as a missionary.

Indigenous religions: a set of beliefs in a supernatural power or powers originating and growing in an area or environment. For example: The term Egyptian religion refers to all aspects of the indigenous religion of ancient Egypt from predynastic times. In some areas, such as much of Africa and Oceana, the indigenous religions are ethnic or tribal; each group has its own particular tradition.

Intercessor: one who prays for the needs of others.

Islam: literally means "submission to the will of Allah (God)."

Islamize: to base laws of society, government, and social and religious behavior on the Qu'ran to the exclusion of all other influences outside of Islam.

Jihad: an Islamic concept often defined as a "holy war" in defense of Islam in militant opposition to any other religion.

Kairos moment: opportune moment.

Lost: spiritual condition of those who have never put their faith in Jesus Christ as their Lord and Savior, who will spend eternity separated from the presence of God.

Maharaj: Hindu prince or leader.

Messianic believer: a Jew who has placed his or her faith in Jesus Christ as the Messiah.

Muslim Background Believer: former Muslim who has placed their faith in Jesus Christ as Lord and Savior.

Nation: people who are defined by a shared history, language, or ethnic link.

Nationals: peoples or ethnic groups of a particular country having a common origin, tradition, and language; indigenous birth or origin in a place or region; people who have always lived in a place, as distinguished from a visitor or a temporary resident or a foreigner.

Palestinian believer: one who lives in the land of Palestine and has placed their faith in Jesus Christ as Lord and Savior.

Palestinian Muslim Background Believer: one who lives in the land of Palestine who formerly was a follower of Islam who has now placed their faith in Jesus Christ as Lord and Savior.

Parachurch ministries: organizations whose primary purpose is to support the Church and help it to carry out the mandate of the Great Commission.

Paradigm: an example or model, from which a class or group may be understood.

Prayer journeyer: one who travels along strategically developed routes, often over long distances, across large territories; prayers are aimed at waging spiritual warfare and establishing the blessing of God throughout specific cities, whole regions, countries, or even continents.

Prayerwalk: walking through a neighborhood, city, or country and praying for the area.

Praying Through The Window—**Calculation of Statistics:** After each *PTTW* initiative, Christian Information Network writes all registered participants and ask them to verify that they in fact prayed. If registrants do not respond after CIN sends multiple letters requesting verification, we count their involvement as "one" even if they reported larger numbers previously. This applies to churches as well as ministries who do not verify their statistics. For instance, in 1993 we attempted to verify a certain ministry's number of participants but did not receive their verification by the time we closed the statistics. Therefore, we counted the ministry's number of participants as "one." When we received their report months later, we learned that the ministry had actually rallied 500,000 believers to pray.

Praying Through The Window: an AD2000 United Prayer Track initiative that began in 1992. The purpose of this prayer initiative is to bring awareness to the Body of Christ worldwide to focus on the 10/40 Window. This awareness has resulted in millions of home-based intercessors praying from their homelands and thousands of prayer journeyers traveling to the Window nations to pray. Prayer for the Window countries occurred during the months of October 1993, 1995, and 1997. The final prayer initiative as we presently know it will be in October of 1999.

Praying Through The Window I: global prayer initiative in October 1993 that focused on 62 countries located in the 10/40 Window (the number changed later to 64).

Praying Through The Window II: global prayer initiative in October 1995 that focused prayer on the 100 Gateway Cities of the 10/40 Window.

Praying Through The Window III: global prayer initiative in October 1997 that focused prayer on the 10/40 Window unreached people groups, most of whom have never heard the Gospel in their own language and in a culturally sensitive way.

Praying Through The Window IV: global prayer initiative in October 1999, which will be the last global prayer effort of AD2000 United Prayer Tract. This prayer initiative focuses once again on the countries of the 10/40 Window.

Qu'ran: book of sacred writings accepted by Muslims as revelations made to Mohammed by Allah through the angel Gabriel.

Ramadan: the ninth month of the Muslim calendar. During this month, Muslims fast daily from food, drink, and sexual intercourse from sunup to sundown.

Tentmakers: those who use their primary vocation in other countries as an avenue to share their faith in Jesus Christ.

Two-thirds World: non-Western nations.

Underevangelized: people who have heard the Gospel to a limited extent.

Unevangelized: people who have never heard the Gospel.

Unreached people groups: those who have yet to hear the Gospel in their own language or presented in a cultural context that they can understand.

World A: as defined by David Barrett, editor of *World Christian Encyclopedia*. "This is a statistical concept with three layers of measurements: World A individuals are unevangelized or unreached, never having heard the name of Jesus Christ, or Christianity, nor the Gospel. World A 'peoples' are ethnolinguistic groups whose number of unevangelized is 50 percent or more. Likewise, World A nations or countries are those with more than 50 percent unevangelized persons." Statistics are based on the enormous United Nations demographic database with its 100 variables for every country in the world for every year from 1950 to 2050, and on David Barrett's religious and Christian data. The formula producing the evangelization analysis includes all obvious Christian variables such as status of print Scripture, *JESUS* film, church members, mission agencies, broadcasting, etc. The map of World A peoples or countries uses a hard black line around the world, somewhat similar to the 10/40 Window but bulging northward include Kazakstan and southward to include Somalia and Indonesia.

APPENDIX

The Evolution of the 10/40 Window Concept

The concept behind the 10/40 Window is not original to us. For many years, various people and ministries have highlighted the location of the peoples most in need of the Gospel.

Almost 90 years ago, Samuel M. Zwemer wrote a book called *The Unoccupied Fields of Africa and Asia*. The cover featured a map of the world highlighting countries that were unoccupied mission fields; most are in the 10/40 Window.

At Lausanne I in 1974, Ralph Winter spoke on cross-cultural evangelism and very casually said, "There are still 2.4 billion people beyond the range of present efforts of any existing church or mission." Billy Graham picked up on this concern during the gathering and said, "It is not enough that we witness to our near neighbors. We must cross cultural and linguistic barriers with the Gospel."

As far back as the early 1980s, David B. Barrett, editor of the *World Christian Encyclopedia*, referred to the least-evangelized people of the globe as "World A" (see glossary). The vast majority of these people, of course, are in the 10/40 Window.

In 1993, Patrick J. Johnstone described this area as the "Resistant Belt" in his book *Operation World*. He noted that it was an area resistant to the claims of Christ, resistant to the advance of the Gospel, and intolerant of those proclaiming the Gospel.

George Otis, Jr. identified an "oval power center" that overlapped a number of the core countries of the 10/40 Window.

It's obvious that the Lord has been directing our attention to this needy area of the world during this century. Where did the name "10/40 Window" come from?

At Lausanne II, held in 1989 in Manila with the theme "The Challenge Before Us," I (Luis) noted that most of the unreached people groups "live in a belt that extends from West Africa across Asia, between ten degrees north to forty degrees north of the equator. This includes the Muslim block, the Hindu block, and the Buddhist block...We must refocus our efforts in evangelization."

Over the following twelve months, as I observed that part of the world both from the outside and from the inside, I became increasingly convinced that we had to focus on this geographic region. On 17 July 1990, at the first meeting of the International Board of the AD 2000 and Beyond Movement, we came to a challenging conclusion: "If we are serious about providing a valid opportunity for every people and city to experience the love, truth, and saving power of Jesus Christ, we cannot ignore the reality that we must concentrate on the resistant region of the world."

We defined this unevangelized/unreached belt as the area "between 10 degrees north and 40 degrees north of the Equator and from West Africa to East Asia," and called it the "10/40 Box." Later, awakening one morning to the beauty of a new day and majestic redwood trees framed by our window, the first words that came to my wife, Doris, and me captured a new idea: "Rather than a 10/40 box, why not think of it as the 10/40 Window? A window is a picture of hope, light, life, and vision."

Later that week, I saw some just-finished software for making and analyzing ministry maps, developed by Pete Holzmann and Strategic Mapping, Inc. I used this software to merge information on the countries in the 10/40 Window, including quality-of-life, percent of known evangelicals, location of non-Christian religions, poverty level, etc.

A few days later, I returned to ask Pete's assistance to create an accurate box on the map, make the calculations, and design maps. When I saw the amazing overlap of the poorest of the poor upon the least evangelized, I fell on my face on the floor in Pete's office because of the confirmation of the picture of need that was emerging.

During this last century of the second millennium, God has been shining His laser-beam on this desperately needy area of the world. It is obviously on His heart. May it be on our hearts, also.

Praying Through The Window Charts

Total number of individual intercessors involved in *Praying Through The Window I, II & III*

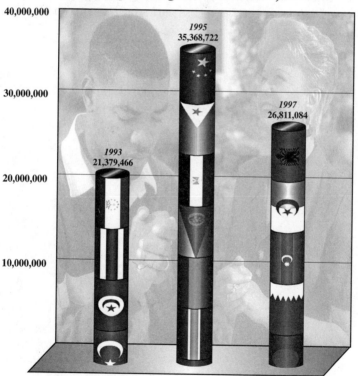

40,000,000

1995
35,368,722

30,000,000

1997
26,811,084

1993
21,379,466

20,000,000

10,000,000

Total number of prayer journeys taken to pray on-site in 10/40 Window nations as part of *Praying Through The Window I, II & III*

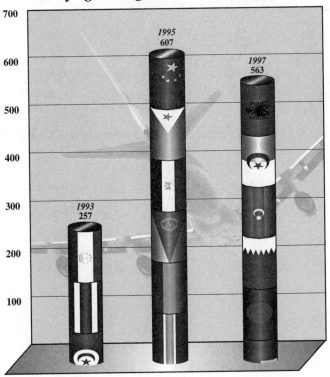

Total number of countries involved in
Praying Through The Window I, II & III

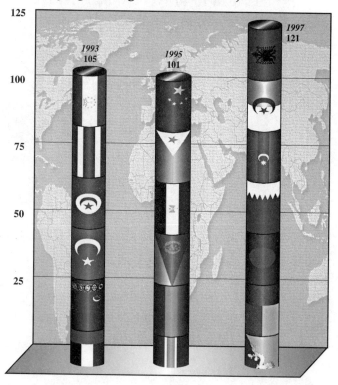

These Groups Can Help You Meet the Challenge

If you desire additional historical and background information or current updates of the changing prayer concerns about the countries, cities, and people groups mentioned in this book, we highly recommend the following organizations and ministries:

AD2000 and Beyond Movement, the world wide movement to establish a church among every people and make the gospel available to every person by the year 2000. 2860 S. Circle Dr, Suite 2112, Colorado Springs, CO 80906, USA. Phone (719) 576-2000; Fax (719) 576-2685; E-mail: info@ad2000.org Web: http://www.ad2000.org

Adopt-A-People, A collecting group of unreached people data. PO Box 17490, Colorado Springs, CO 80935-7490, USA. Phone (719) 574-7001.

AIMS Global Information Center, Association of International Mission Services, North American Office, PO Box 64534, Virginia Beach, VA 23464, USA. Phone (804) 579-5850; Fax (804) 579-5851; E-mail: aims@cbn.org

Anglican Frontier Missions, PO Box 18024, Richmond VA 23226, USA. Phone (804) 355-8468; E-mail: AFM@xc.org

Asian Minorities Outreach, assists in the salvation of Asia's ethnic minorities who are the most unreached and the least helped. Box 17, Chang Klan P.O., Chiang Mai 50100, Thailand. Phone (66-53) 281-778; Fax (66-53)281-778; E-mail: cnxphttw@cmu.chiangmai.ac.th

Asian Outreach, Dr. David Wang. GPO box 3448, Hong Kong. Phone (852) 288-59555; Fax (852) 256-79016

Bethany World Prayer Center, In Baton Rouge, Louisiana, USA. Has unreached people groups prayer profiles to complete and produce for distribution to praying churches and individuals. Attention: Unreached Peoples Project, 13855 Plank Rd, Baker, LA 70714, USA. Phone (504) 664-2000; Fax (504) 774-2001; E-mail: 102132.52@ Compuserve.com. Web:http://www.goshen.net/calebproject/upg.pray.htw

Blessings International, Medicine for missions in developing nations, PO Box 35292, Tulsa OK 741543-0292, USA. Phone (918) 250-8101

Bridges for Peace, Assistance and food bank for those in need, especially the elderly, in Jerusalem. PO Box 33145, Tulsa, OK 74153, USA. Phone: (918) 461-8800.

Caleb Project, 10 West Dry Creek Circle, Littleton, CO 80120, USA. Phone (303) 730-4170; Fax (303) 730-4177; E-mail AdvoNet@cproject.com. Web: http://www.goshen.net/calebproject

Campus Crusade for Christ, 100 Sunport Lane, Orlando, Fl 32809. Phone (407) 826-2833; Fax (407) 826-2851

Centre for Mission Direction, PO Box 31-146, Christchurch 8030 New Zealand. Phone (03) 342-7711; Fax (03) 342-8410; E-mail: Info@cmd.org.nz. Bob Hall internet, b.hall@soci.canterbury.ac.nz

Christ For India, PO Box 271086, Dallas TX 75227, USA. Phone (214) 771-7221, Fax (214) 771-4021

Christian Broadcasting Network, 977 Centerville Turnpike, Virginia Beach, VA, USA 23463-0001. Phone (757) 579-7000

Christian Friends of Israel Community Development Foundation (ICDF), PO Box 16050, Colorado Springs CO 80935, USA. Phone (719) 380-7188; E-mail: Tedbecket@aol.com

Christian Information Network, Beverly Pegues, Executive Director for the Praying Through The Window projects. 11005 Highway 83 N., Suite 159, Colorado Springs, CO 80921, USA. Phone (719) 522-1040; Fax (719) 277-7148; E-mail: cin@cin1040.net, Web: www.christian-info.com

Christian Solidarity International, Zelglistrasse 64, PO Box 70, CH-8122 Binz by Zurich, Switzerland, Phone 41-1-980-47-00; Fax 41-1-980-15; E-mail: csi-int@csi-int.ch. Web: http://www.csi-int.ch

Christians for Israel USA, PO Box 72, Star Tannery, VA 22654-0072, USA. Phone (540)436-3600; Fax (540) 459-3608; E-mail: chfisrus@shentel.net

Dawn Ministries, 7899 Lexington Dr. Suite 200-B, Colorado Springs, CO 80920, USA. Phone (719) 548-7460; Fax 719-548-7475; E-mail: 767731,2145@compuserv.com

End-Time Handmaidens, Inc., PO Box 447, Jasper, Arizona 72641, USA. Phone (501) 446-2252; Fax (501) 446-2259

Engineering Ministries International, 110 S Weber Suite 104, Colorado Springs, CO 80903-1934. Phone (719) 633-2078; Fax (719) 633-2970

Every Home for Christ, Dick Eastman, International President. PO Box 35930, Colorado Springs, CO 80935-3593, USA. Phone (719) 260-8888; Fax (719) 260-7505

Freedom House, 120 Wall Street, New York, NY 10005, USA. Phone (212) 514-8040; Fax (212) 514-8045; E-mail: frhouse@freedomhouse.org

Frontier Ventures, Mobilizing prayer for the world's unreached peoples and mobilizing prayer for laborers on the world's spiritual frontiers. PO Box 49757, Colorado Springs, CO 80949, USA. Phone (719)594-2481; Fax (719) 598-4063.

Friendship International Ministries, Inc.,
Interdenominational ministry through The Friends' Church, focuses on a desire to meet the needs of people in Eastern Europe through spiritual, intellectual and physical levels. Del Huff, PO Box 50884, Colorado Springs, CO 80909, USA. Phone (719) 386-8808.

Generals of Intercession, Mike & Cindy Jacobs, Co-Founders, PO Box 49788, Colorado Springs, CO 80949-9788, USA. Phone (719) 535-0977; Fax (719)535-0884

Servants Fellowship International, Bringing Hope to Suffering Christians in the Muslim World. Dr. Patrick Sookhdeo, St. Andrew's Centre, St. Andrew's Road, Plaistow, London E13 8QD United Kingdom.

Global Evangelization Movement (GEM), David Barrett, PO Box 6628, Richmond, VA 23230, USA.
Web: http://www.gem-werc.org/materials.htm

Global Harvest Ministries, C. Peter and Doris M. Wagner, PO Box 63060, Colorado Springs, CO 80962, USA. Phone (719) 262-9922; Fax (719) 262-9920;
E-mail: 74114.570@compuserve.com

Great Commission Center, 769 Orchid Hill Lane, Argyle (Copper Canyon), TX 76226, USA. E-mail: 74513.3361@compuserve.com. Or Hong Kong Plaza, Suite 2716, 186-191 Cannaught Road West, Shek Tong Tsui, Hong Kong. Fax (852) 2540-9770

India Mission Association, 48.I Main Road, East Shenoy Nagar, PO Box 2529, Madras 600 030, INDIA.
Phone 044-617596; Fax 044-611859

Institute for the Study of Islam and Christianity, St Andrew's Centre, St Andrew's Road, Plaistow, London, UK E13 8QD.
E-mail: 101376.2103@compuserve.com

International Aviation Embassy, PO Box 1192, Jerusalem 91010, ISRAEL

International Bible Society, 1820 Jet Stream Drive, Colorado Springs, CO 80921-3696, USA. Phone (719) 488-9200

International Day of Prayer for the Persecuted Church, Steve Haas. PO Box WEF, Wheaton, IL 60189-0498.
Phone (800) 538-7772; Fax (800) 668-0498

International Ministries, Presenting A-Risen Christ Today, PO Box 2500, Redmond WA 98073-2500, USA.
Phone (206) 882-0761

International Needs, Helping Christians serve God in their own countries, International Office, 20210 84th Ave, Langley B.C. V2Y 2B7 Canada, or USA, PO Box 977, Lynden WA 98264, USA. Phone (604) 888-5558; Fax (604) 888-5919; Web: http://www.ualberta.ca/~dharapnu/intlneed

International Prayer Strategy Office, Foreign Mission Board, Southern Baptist Convention, PO Box 6767, Richmond, VA 23230-0767, USA. Phone (800) 866-3621 or (804) 219-1000

International Students Inc, Tom Phillips, 2863 South Circle Dr. Suite 600, Colorado Springs, CO 80906-4112, USA.
Phone (719) 576-2700; Fax (719) 576-5363

Iranian Christian International, Inc., An international organization that ministers to Iranians, Afghans and other Persian speaking people. PO Box 25607, Colorado Springs, CO 80936, USA. Phone (719) 596-0010.

Joshua Project 2000 Unreached Peoples List, 2860 S. Circle Dr., Suite 2112, Colorado Springs, CO 80906, USA.
Phone (719) 576-2000; Fax (719) 576-2685;
E-mail: info@ad2000.org

Manna Church and Ministries, Michael Fletcher, 5117 Cliffdale, Rd., Fayetteville, NC 28314, USA. Phone (910) 867-9151; Fax (910) 867-1737;
E-mail: 102575.1436@compuserve.com

Mission of Mercy, Meeting spiritual and physical needs of hurting people in poverty stricken areas of the world. Through emergency and support roles, people receive food, education, medical aid and the Gospel message. Donald Beard, President, 1465 Kelly Johnson Blvd., Suite 200, Colorado Springs, CO 80920, USA. Phone (719) 593-0099.

Mission to Unreached Peoples, PO Box 45880, Seattle WA 98145-0880, USA. Phone (206) 524-4600; Fax (206) 524-6992

Musalaha, Salim Munayer, Director. PO Box 127, Bethlehem, West Bank, ISRAEL

The Network for Strategic Missions, Executive Director, P.O. Box 6543, Virginia Beach, VA 23456. Phone (757) 226-5001; Fax (757) 226-5006; E-mail: thenetworkio@compuserve.com

Operation Reach All International, PO Box 64154, Virginia Beach VA 23467, USA. Phone (757) 497-9320; Fax (757) 497-9352; E-mail: ora@infi.net

Operation Reveille, Bruce Sidebotham. 3969 Half Turn Place, Colorado Springs, CO 80917. Phone (719) 592-2908

Pray for China Fellowship, OMF International, 10 West Dry Creek Circle, Littleton, Colorado 80120-4413, USA

Salvation Air Force, To provide aviation training and support for both home and foreign missions. 3210 East Lasalle Street, Colorado Springs, CO 80909, USA. Phone (719) 633-2369.

Sammy Tippit Ministries, PO Box 460328, San Antonio TX 78246, USA

The Sentinel Group, National prayer profiles covering more than sixty countries within the greater 10/40 Window. George Otis, Jr., PO Box 6334, Lynnwood, WA 98036, USA. Phone (206) 627-2989; Fax (206) 672-3028.

The Sowers Ministry, 154 Prince Edward Road, 4/F, Kowloon, Hong Kong. Phone: 671-0460; Fax 668-0407

Training Evangelistic Leadership (TEL), TEL, PO Drawer E, Denton TX 76202, USA. Phone (817) 382-8365 or 321-3913.

Hong Kong address: CPO Box 737759, Kowloon, Hong Kong. Phone (852) 2983-2240 or (852) 2496-1279

U.S. Center for World Mission, Ralph Winter, 1605 E. Elizabeth St, Pasadena, CA 91104-9969, USA. Phone (818) 798-0819

United Mission to Muslims Alliance, The AD2000 Muslim Task Force. Frontiers 325 N. Stapley Drive, Mesa, AZ, 85203, USA

Voice of the Martyrs, Worldwide information on those persecuted for their Christian faith .PO Box 443, Bartlesville, OK 74005, Phone (918) 337-8015; Fax (918) 337-9287.

Voice of Truth, PO Box 15013, Colorado Springs, CO 80935 USA. Phone (719) 574-5900; Fax (719) 574-6075

World by 2000, Committed to provide the Gospel by radio in every language. 7899 Lexington Dr., Suite 200-B, Colorado Springs, CO 80918, USA. Phone (719) 548-7490.

World Impact, Foursquare Missions International, 1910 West Sunset Blvd., Suite 200, Los Angeles, CA 90026, USA. Phone (213) 484-2400, ext. 327; Fax (213) 483-5863

World Vision International, 800 W. Chestnut Avenue, Monrovia, CA 91016, USA. Phone (626) 303-8811, Fax (626) 301-7786

Youth With A Mission International (YWAM), PO Box 26479, Colorado Springs, CO 80936, USA. Phone (719) 380-0505; Fax (719) 380-0936

Youth With A Mission Strategic Frontiers, Fred Markert. PO Box 25490, Colorado Springs, CO 80936. Phone (719) 527-9594; Fax (719) 527-2680

About the Authors

Born in Argentina and raised in Brazil, **Luis Bush** studied theology in Texas after three years in business accounting and systems work. Upon graduation from seminary, he and his wife, Doris, moved to El Salvador, where he pastored Iglesia Nazaret, a mushrooming mission-focused church in San Salvador. In the seven years he served as pastor, the church grew to almost 1,300, and the congregation planted seven daughter churches and supported over 35 missionaries.

From 1986 to March 1992, Bush served as chief executive officer of Partners International (PI), which is associated with almost 70 indigenous ministries in 50 countries. During his tenure, he served as congress director for COMIBAM/Nov. 87, an Ibero-American consultation for 3,000 leaders from throughout Latin America moving from a mission field to a mission force. Also, the associated partner ministries of PI established over 2,800 new churches, 80 percent of which were in the 10/40 Window.

Bush pinpointed the need for a major focus of evangelism in the "10/40 Window," a phrase he coined in his presentation at the Lausanne II Conference in Manila, in July 1989. This concept led to *Praying Through The Window I* in October 1993 with an approximate 21 million participants, *Praying Through The Window II* in October 1995 involving some 35 million intercessors, *Praying Through The Window III* in October 1997, and *Praying Through The Window IV* in October 1999.

Presently Bush is involved in encouraging the implementation of countrywide initiatives focused on the unfinished task and implementing a strategy to establish a church planting movement among each of the world's least evangelized peoples called "Joshua Project 2000." This plan emerged out of the Global Consultation on World Evangelization (GCOWE '95) which was held in May 1995 in Seoul, Korea, and drew 4,000 participants in the AD2000 and Beyond Movement from 186 countries. Bush served as senior consultant to GCOWE '97 which was held in Pretoria, South Africa, from June 30 to July 5, 1997, and drew 4,000 participants in the AD2000 and Beyond Movement from 130 countries.

Luis Bush and his wife, Doris, have four children and live in Colorado Springs, Colorado.

Beverly Pegues is the executive director of the Christian Information Network. CIN administers and facilitates AD2000 United Prayer Track's *Praying Through The Window* prayer initiatives. A career paralegal turned mission agency administrator, Pegues also organizes prayer for New Life Church, where she is a member and serves as the missions director.

Pegues attended the University of Colorado at Colorado Springs (UCCS) and also earned a paralegal certificate from UCCS. She has taken numerous law office management and paralegal classes from Denver University School of Law and Continuing Legal Education of Colorado as well as various management classes from Pikes Peak Community College. Pegues is the founder and director of a youth-based performing arts group, The Academy of Black Arts. She is also the recipient of the Woman of the Year Award from the Colorado Black Women for Political Action and a member of the International Third World Conference.

The primary author of *WindoWatchman I,* Pegues is the editor of *WindoWatchman II.* These books document the signs, wonders, and miracles the Lord performed during the *Praying Through The Window* initiatives in the lives of both the people in the 10/40 Window nations and the prayer journeyers as well as in the lives of home-based intercessors.

Beverly speaks at conferences, churches, and retreats nationally and internationally. She has spoken in several countries, including Germany, Jordan, Egypt, Korea, Sweden, and Lebanon. Her delightful personality reflects the warmth and love of Jesus as she ministers on subjects from prayer, praise, and worship to maturing in our faith.

Beverly Pegues and her husband, Leonard, live in Colorado Springs, Colorado. Their adult daughter, LaTonya, lives in Southern California.